Thriving in the Age of Chronic Illness

All the best!

Jason Reid

Thriving in the Age of Chronic Illness

Sick with Success ®
663 Montbeck Cr.
Mississauga Ontario.
L5G 1P1

This book should not be used to diagnose or treat any illness
be it mental or physical. Always seek qualified medical
advice. The author and publisher are not responsible for the
use or misuse of any information contained in this book.

Sick with Success®

Sick with Success® provides information, personalized
coaching, keynote presentations and leadership training in
the areas of chronic illness, engagement and productivity.
For more information on one-on-one coaching or hiring
Jason Reid as a speaker you can email us at
info@sickwithsuccess.com. You can also order more books
by calling 905.891.3584. Discounts are available on large
orders.

ISBN – 978-1-77084-129-1

Printed in Canada
♻
on recycled paper

FIRST CHOICE BOOKS
DEMAND PUBLISHING & BINDING

www.firstchoicebooks.ca
Victoria, BC

10 9 8 7 6 5 4 3 2

Thriving in the Age of Chronic Illness

A guide for people with chronic health conditions and the organizations that employ them.

by

Jason Reid

Sick with Success®
www.sickwithsuccess.com

Acknowledgements

I am indebted to many people for both their help and their support over the past two years. There are far too many names to mention here, but they know who they are and I could not have put together this book without them.

I would particularly like to thank Susan Adsett, who not only designed the cover and acted as copy editor, but also encouraged and supported me from the very beginning. I would also like to acknowledge my furry feline companion Wellington who kept me company during long hours at the computer and always reminded me to take appropriate breaks. He did this important work while fighting his own serious illness. His grandmother would be proud of him.

Table of contents

Jason Reid

Thriving in the Age of Chronic Illness

Preface

This book started as a compilation of several dozen articles written over the past two years on the subject of chronic illness, success and employee engagement. During the process of editing however, I felt the need to add several more chapters for context and eliminated others that seemed redundant. I reworked each and every article, shortening some and extending others, to the point where the book is now a completely new creation.

One thing I did not change was the short, breezy style of each of the chapters. They still read like self-contained essays, which makes the content easier to grasp and allows readers to use this like a reference book.

Whenever you have a spare moment, you can pick up the book, invest a couple minutes in a chapter, and then go about the rest of your day with a new idea or perspective to think about.

The book has two primary audiences: individual people who are challenged by chronic health conditions and the organizations that employ them. It is my opinion that each can learn something from understanding the other's point of view. In fact, bridging the gap of understanding is primarily what this book is about.

Part I looks at the specific characteristics that define chronic illness and how these characteristics differ from our assumptions. *Part II* looks at chronic illness issues from a business and organizational perspective. The final section is aimed at helping individuals who are challenged by chronic illness become more engaged in their lives and careers.

Please keep in mind that I am not a medical doctor and the contents of this book should not be used to diagnose or treat any disease. It is also important to be aware of employment laws and abide by them, particularly as they relate to employee confidentiality and privacy.

Introduction

I have been looking for a book like this for years. The fact that no one else has written one up to now is one of the primary reasons I created my coaching and training company, *Sick with Success®*, which focuses primarily on the engagement of people working and living with chronic illnesses.

Sick with Success® stems from the idea that there are many people with chronic health conditions who are smart, ambitious and want to be successful in their careers. The key to success is engagement, but the assumptions and stereotypes which fuel government and corporate policies often get in the way of such engagement.

Then there is the issue of resources. Where can these people go for advice when dealing with the life challenges related to working with a chronic health condition? Most commonly, they have to rely on support groups or mental health professionals. These resources have their limits.

Many ambitious people dislike support groups – referring to them as *pity parties*. Predictably, a group dynamic that is built primarily around problems rather than strengths and solutions has the unfortunate tendency to keep people where they are rather than helping them move on.

As a one-on-one resource, mental health professionals serve an important purpose in our society and are a valuable lifeline for those with emotional or psychological problems. However, not everyone who has a chronic illness needs psychological therapy or wants it.

Personally, I found that the problems I faced as an ambitious person with a chronic illness could not be fully understood by people who did not have first-hand experience in the real world. I felt that a new type of resource was needed.

At the time, I was working as a news director for a national television network. It was a job that involved long hours and a lot of pressure, but it was also fun and rewarding. I worked with some very talented journalists, writers and technical staff. These people were in similarly stressful jobs, and many had their own chronic health problems. These conditions included cancer, arthritis, depression, and inflammatory bowel disease (just to name a few). I also had employees whose lives were affected by the serious health conditions of close family members as well.

In fact, most people in my department seemed to be affected by chronic illness, either directly or indirectly. I thought this was rare until I discovered that a third of the workforce has at least one chronic health condition. It turned out that the number of sick people in my department was not rare at all. It was *normal*.

The key difference was that my employees actually *told me* about their health challenges rather than keeping them a secret. Most of them knew I had a chronic illness myself and looked to me for both understanding and also ways to improve their productivity. Many managers never hear about their employee's health conditions. I was an exception.

As a result, I began looking for resources that could help me better engage employees with chronic illness issues. There was nothing out there. No books. No workshops, and almost no experts. The idea seemed to be if you got sick you left your ambition behind, exited the workforce or fell back on an entry level job that required little thought or effort.

After years of seeking out resources that would help ill employees, I realized that I might have to create them myself. After all, I had been working my entire life with two painful and sometimes serious conditions: Crohn's disease – an inflammatory bowel condition, and arthritis – which made my body ache and occasionally swelled up my knees and ankles to near comic proportions.

Despite my physical challenges, I had succeeded in one of the most competitive industries in the world: television news. I had also done it in a way that reflected my own personal values. I treated people as individuals and emphasized their unique strengths. Every person brought something different and powerful to the team and respected each other's differences. Recognizing people as individuals also meant recognizing their different needs, so being flexible and meeting those needs was an important part of my management philosophy

As I gained experience as a manager, I began to appreciate the positive impact this philosophy had on my employees who were challenged by illness issues. Productivity in key areas was soon quadruple what it had been when I took over the department and the quality of work being produced was never better. For the first time in their careers, my staff were winning national and international journalism awards and beating the biggest names in television news around the world.

I believe this happened, in large part, due to the level of trust, understanding, and flexibility I incorporated into the workplace. My employees knew I understood their health and family challenges and would do everything I could to get them the resources they needed to do their jobs better.

They also knew my commitment to excellence. Having a chronic health condition does not mean you stop caring about the quality of your work. However, it should make you aware of where to spend your energy, when to take a break and how to balance your life. It is about creating priorities and making good decisions. When people feel a pride in what they do, and do it in a way that nourishes them physically and mentally, they become truly *engaged* in their work. And when employees are engaged, they are also highly productive.

Acting as a catalyst for engagement soon became the most rewarding part of my job, and seeing the positive impact it had on the bottom line was an inspiration in itself. If I could help my team increase productivity and quality so substantially and so quickly, why couldn't I teach those skills to others?

After all, I know the fears, the challenges and the difficult decisions that come from being an ambitious person with a chronic illness.

Having been a manager, I also know the challenges, concerns and difficult decisions that come with responsibility, as well as the frustrations of dealing with corporate policies that exist for a reason, but are not always effective at getting the results that we want.

I chose the title of this book deliberately. Having spent the past two years studying data on chronic illness and productivity, I now believe this issue has as large an impact on our society as the *Age of Industry*, the *Age of Information* or the *Age of Globalization*.

The rise of chronic illness is an elephant in the room that few leaders want to truly acknowledge. Our world has been affected by major changes in demographics and medicine that have literally transformed the very concept of illness itself. Until we come to grips with these fundamental transformations, we will spend money, time and effort on strategies that no longer work for anyone.

The purpose of this book is to identify and change many of the underlying assumptions we have about illness and start a new dialogue that will lead to more effective solutions for both organizations and individuals.

PART I – WHAT IS CHRONIC ILLNESS?

Over the past few generations there has been a seismic shift in the way people become ill. Throughout most of human history, bacteria and viruses were the main cause of sickness. They brought about deadly diseases such as plague, tuberculosis and diphtheria. By the late 20th century things had changed. Many of these highly contagious diseases had been controlled or eliminated through the use of antibiotics and vaccines.

Today, the primary cause of death and disability comes from *chronic* illnesses – diseases that are generally not contagious, but are often incurable. Chronic illness is not a diagnosis in itself, but a term that describes the long-term nature of the disease.

There is some debate in medical circles over exactly which diseases qualify, but the next chapter will give you a practical way of understanding what chronic illness looks like. There are also resources at the back of the book that highlight the many different chronic diseases that now affect much of our population.

Defining chronic illness in a few letters

When we think about common health problems we often consider things like the flu, respiratory infections, viruses and broken bones. These are all conditions that are visible, temporary and predictable. These are also known as *acute* conditions and throughout the course of human history they have generally been responsible for the majority of our health problems.

Due to our aging population and advances in medical technology (which keep more people alive and productive) the majority of the world's health-care issues are no longer acute, but *chronic*. In fact, *The World Health Organization* recognizes more than 70 different types of chronic disease, and states that chronic illness is now the leading cause of death and disability in the world.

If we look at the different characteristics of both acute and chronic disease, we will see that the paradigm of illness has changed dramatically.

The word *acute* means urgent or severe. The course of an acute illness has the following general characteristics:

- **Predictable** - Acute illness follows a predictable course. You either fight off the infection or you die.
- **Visible** – Most acute illnesses (even something like the flu) are visible. You can tell when someone is sick.

- **Temporary** – Acute illnesses are usually of relatively short duration.

Now let us look at the characteristics of chronic illness. The word *chronic* means long-term. An easy way to remember the characteristics of chronic illness is by using the acronym U-ILL (Think of it as a question: *You ill?*). The letters stand for:

- **Unpredictable** – Symptoms can often flare up or recede quickly and without warning.
- **Invisible** – Most people with chronic illness show no obvious signs of being ill and look "normal".
- **Long Lasting** – Many chronic diseases are incurable.

Contrast these elements with the predictable, visible and temporary nature of acute illness, and you can appreciate the problem we have with our assumptions about what it means to be sick. The whole paradigm of illness has changed.

Unfortunately, the tools we use to address illness are still rooted in the past. Think about your short-term disability policies or return to work strategies. Do they make assumptions that an employee's illness will run a predictable course which will see them get better over a period of time until the point where they are fully well again? Similar assumptions are at the heart of almost all of our institutions and policies that relate to people and their health - encompassing everything from our medical system to our social safety net and even to collective bargaining agreements.

Human health has a huge impact on our society and the economy. If our assumptions about what it means to be sick are wildly out of date, how can we properly address the problems and issues of our workforce and our citizens?

Unpredictable

For people with a chronic illness, getting well is not just a simple case of getting some rest and going to the doctor. Chronic diseases can be highly unpredictable. Flare-ups and remissions can happen almost at random, while symptoms such as pain and fatigue can change from day to day or even hour to hour. To add to the uncertainty, many people who are challenged by a chronic health condition actually have more than one disease. This often leads to an unpredictable soup of symptoms that can be tough to predict. It may also explain why people with chronic diseases are much more likely to suffer from depression than the normal population.

I know from personal experience how difficult it is to adjust to this uncertainty. I have gone through many periods where my health seemed to change almost daily. One of my toughest stretches was a ten-year phase where I would suddenly, and without warning, become stricken with a high-grade fever. I would literally end up flat on my back for more than a week each time it happened. Despite numerous emergency room visits, the doctors could not explain why this was occurring. They just knew it was somehow related to my Crohn's disease.

Because the fevers were wildly unpredictable, I was unable to book a holiday abroad, commit to social events or even know with confidence that I would be able to work the next day. It was like my body was a time bomb and I never knew when it would go off. The situation frayed my nerves and made it almost impossible to relax even when I was feeling okay. I could never plan anything nice for myself and I was constantly worried about my ability to keep my job amid mounting sick time. This stressful situation continued for a decade.

Eventually, I was put on a new medication and my fevers mysteriously disappeared, but it took me more than a year to feel any sort of freedom again. Even now, with the fevers behind me, I still don't know from each day to the next how much energy I will have or how much pain I will feel, but I have learned to adapt as best as I can. Such is life with a chronic illness.

Invisible

The vast majority of people with chronic diseases (96%) have no visible symptoms. For those who suffer from these conditions, this invisibility can have serious effects on their relationships with others.

Most of us expect sickness to be visible. So when someone tells us they are ill, but they don't look sick, we assume they are exaggerating or being untruthful.

Imagine having a serious health problem, or a serious problem of *any* kind and having no one believe you. Imagine if this was part of your everyday life.

One would think that doctors would be immune to these assumptions, but sometimes they are not. When I was eight years old I started feeling waves of pain in my gut. I knew there was something seriously wrong, but no one believed me. The doctor could not *see* my illness – so to him it didn't exist. Instead of getting help, I was labeled a troubled child and told that the pain was all in my head. After two years of pleading I was finally admitted to hospital and diagnosed with Crohn's disease – an inflammatory bowel condition which, at that time, was rare among children.

Two years is a long time to a child. Two years of not being believed by someone in authority was devastating to me. I was always told that doctors were there to help me and that they knew everything. Why did they accuse me of *lying*?

Things got worse as I got older. When I was in my early twenties I starting taking medication that gave me painful kidney stones. As a result, I would often end up in the emergency room in need of a shot of morphine. On one memorable occasion, I was taken by ambulance to a hospital in one of the rougher areas of the city. When the emergency room doctor looked at me, he noticed I was young, pale and thin, but looked healthy otherwise. He made the assumption I was a drug abuser and was faking symptoms to get pain medication.

This was not the last time I was mistaken for a drug addict. In fact, I started dreading the emergency room visits even more than the kidney stones. Imagine being in agony and having a nurse threaten to throw you out of the hospital. Picture being *laughed at* by a doctor who refuses to give you morphine, as you lie screaming in pain on a stretcher. This is the type of situation I dealt with on a regular basis and I know I am not alone. Many others have told me similar stories of being misunderstood by the very people they trusted to help them. Whether it's a doctor, boss, friend or spouse, having someone disbelieve you when you are sick is an unpleasant experience.

Regrettably, these sad misunderstandings can build up over time and gradually erode the type of trust that is crucial to developing good relationships.

I was reminded of this recently when I came across a great quote from renowned life coach Tony Robbins. He was describing what happens to people who are abused as children, but his statement also describes the social effects of living with an invisible illness.

He said: *"When people become wounded and not helped by others they start to feel that real communication is not possible."*

When others are wounded and seek *your* understanding will you treat them with suspicion or with empathy? Your decision can have far-reaching effects either way.

Invisibility makes communication difficult, but not impossible. In order for us to truly understand people with chronic illness, we have to be receptive and willing to listen.

Long lasting

Many people still have trouble grasping the concept of a *long term* or *incurable* illness. After all, most of us grew up with the idea that doctors could fix everything, right?

When you get diagnosed with a chronic illness you learn pretty quickly about the limits of a doctor's curative power. Doctors become people who treat symptoms and try to limit long-term damage rather than cure us from disease.

Having an illness that will stay with you for the rest of your life is a scary thought, but it is surprising how quickly people can adapt to the concept. What seems scary at first eventually becomes normal.

That being said, there are areas where having a long-term condition can have a serious effect over time. Chronic pain and fatigue are two of the most challenging factors. Being in pain day-after-day-after-day can physically change your brain, causing the frontal lobes to *shrink,* affecting everything from your memory to your problem-solving abilities. Chronic fatigue can do the same thing.

There is no doubt that a long-term illness can really wear you down over time. It is like running in a marathon and twisting your knee during the first mile. With each step forward you feel the pain. At certain points during the marathon, your adrenaline might kick in and distract you from the hurt, but the pain eventually comes back full force.

Eventually, all you can think about is reaching the finish line and being done with it.

For some of us though, there is no finish line. This is the way we will spend the rest of their lives. Over time, we develop the mental toughness of the long distance runner and continue moving forward. Despite these considerable challenges, our biggest problem with long-term illness is often the people who think we should just go to the doctor and get cured already. I wish it were that simple.

Part II – THE BUSINESS SIDE OF CHRONIC ILLNESS

If you manage more than a handful of employees, chances are that some of them are challenged by a chronic disease. In fact, we know that one in three workers have at least one chronic health condition.

A recent study in Great Britain indicated that most employees with chronic illnesses do not properly maintain their health at work. This may be due to a number of factors, ranging from the stigma attached to illness to a lack of flexibility in their jobs. As chronic health conditions become more prevalent in our society, it is crucial that the workplace provides a supportive atmosphere that allows employees to both maintain their health and take advantage of resources such as wellness programs and flexible work arrangements.

A flexible, understanding culture, which allows employees to perform at their best, will ultimately reduce costs such as absenteeism and presenteeism (employees who show up to work, but are not fully functional). As you will soon see, these costs are a lot higher than you may think.

Just the facts

57.3 million working-aged Americans, 33 percent of the working-aged population, have at least one chronic condition.
Center for Studying Health System Change 2009

Chronic health conditions cost the U.S. economy more than $1 trillion a year, a figure that could jump to nearly $6 trillion by 2050.
Milken Institute. An Unhealthy America: The Economic Burden of Chronic Disease

More than half of Canadians live with a chronic disease.
Canadian Coalition for Public Health in the 21st Century

Worldwide, chronic diseases have overtaken infectious diseases as the leading cause of death and disability. In Ontario, chronic diseases account for 55% of direct and indirect health costs.
Ontario (Canada) Ministry of Health and Long-Term Care May 2007

The economic burden of chronic diseases has been estimated at over $150 billion in direct and indirect costs annually. The cost of lost productivity due to short-term and long-term

disability alone represents close to 30% of total costs. ($50 billion)
Centre for Chronic Disease Prevention and Control. Public Health Agency of Canada

96% of people with chronic illness show no visible symptoms. These people do not use a cane or any assistive device and may look perfectly healthy.
United States Census Bureau 2002

Depression is 15-20% higher for the chronically ill than for the average person
Rifkin, A. "Depression in Physically Ill Patients," 1992

In 1999, the Employers Health Coalition in Florida analyzed seventeen diseases and found that lost productivity from presenteeism was 7.5 times greater than productivity loss from absenteeism. For specific problems, like allergies, arthritis, heart disease, hypertension, migraines, and neck or back pain, the ratio was more than 15 to 1.
The Changing Face of U.S. Health Care: Employers Health Coalition Inc; 1999.

The trillion dollar problem

More than a trillion dollars. That's how much chronic illnesses cost organizations in the United States in 2007. These numbers are expected to *quadruple* by 2030.

A trillion dollars makes the mind boggle. That's a million million. With that amount of money you could pay *all* of the rent cheques in United States for *three years*!

You would think with so much at stake that our business and political leaders would take more of an interest in better engaging people with chronic illness. Not all of this money needs to be lost.

A significant amount of this trillion-dollar productivity loss is due to presenteeism, where people show up for work but are not productive during their time on the job. While many companies track *absenteeism* quite closely, the quality and quantity of the work and the engagement of the employee are not always measured.

To illustrate why this is a problem, let us look at a 2010 survey of chronically ill workers in Canada. The study was called *Patient's Voice* and it was published through *Benefits Canada Magazine*. In it, 80 percent of chronically ill workers that were surveyed said they went into work even when they were not feeling well.

This shocked a doctor on the expert panel that analyzed the data, but I don't think this surprises anyone who has had a serious chronic illness. The fact is that many of us come into work sick because it is expected of us and taking too many days off can quickly kill a promising career.

In our North American culture, there is often skepticism about workers who call in sick more than a few days a year. The assumption is that these workers are uncommitted or lazy.

While there are some people who may take sick days when they are not truly sick, we know that the opposite is also true. Many employees come into work beset by issues such as pain, fatigue and nausea that may significantly affect their productivity on the job.

Here are some additional challenges that contribute to the trillion-dollar problem:

- Chronic illnesses are often invisible.
- Employees generally do not tell their employers about their illness because they worry about being stigmatized or losing their jobs.
- Many of these same people do not monitor or attend to their illness (i.e. take their proper medications etc.) while at work.
- Many organizations are still slow to offer flexible, results-oriented work arrangements that will allow employees to work more efficiently.

We know that chronic illness currently keeps many employees from being fully engaged and productive. However, by finding ways to better engage these employees, organizations can realize significant savings going forward.

One-third of the workforce and growing

In North America, people with chronic health conditions are becoming the majority. According to *The Canadian Coalition for Public Health in the 21st Century* more than half of all Canadians of all ages have at least one chronic illness. Of course, that number includes both the very young and the very old. The number of *working-aged* people with chronic health conditions is smaller but still significant.

In 2009, the American government did a major study on health and wellness. They found that 33 percent of the working-aged population (18 to 64 years old) had at least one chronic health condition. Canadian studies of this age group have come up with similar numbers.

Let's translate these percentages into your own workplace. Think of the number of people in your organization. If you belong to a large organization then you might want to think of the number of people who work in your department instead. Now divide that number by three. This represents how many people in your organization or department likely have a chronic health condition.

When most people do this exercise, they are usually surprised by how large this number is. Why is this? Well there is a gap between what we statistically know is true and what we *perceive* based on our own experience. In this case, we usually discover someone has a chronic illness only when they tell us, because chronic illness is largely invisible. Of course, people will not always tell their employers or co-workers this information because they are afraid of discrimination, loss of future opportunities and possibly even termination.

As a result, it is common for organizations to ignore the chronic illness problem - even as productivity costs start to mount.

Ultimately, the fear of discrimination remains one of the most powerful obstacles to engaging people with chronic illness. What is your organization doing to lessen that fear?

Leadership in the age of chronic illness

Leadership is a word that gets used a lot in the corporate world. There are shelves upon shelves of books on this topic in the business section of any large bookstore. The current flood of information about leadership has actually made defining leadership difficult. Why? Because much of what passes for leadership is actually management.

Management and leadership are both necessary for the success of any organization, but they are different tools for different needs.

The difference between leadership and management

In June of 2011 I was lucky enough to take the executive leadership course from the Marshall School of Business at USC. The course was taught by leadership expert and best-selling author Dr. Dave Logan. We spent a lot of time identifying the crucial differences between management and leadership. I offer a brief summary:

What is management?

Management involves areas such as planning and budgeting, organization and staffing, controlling and problem solving. The focus of management is to produce predictability and order, with the purpose of generating the short-term results expected by stakeholders.

What is leadership?

Leadership is about establishing a vision and strategy, then communicating in words and deeds so that everyone aligns to and understands that vision and strategy. Leadership should energize people to overcome bureaucratic barriers to change. The purpose of leadership is to produce a dramatic change in approach, which has the potential to create value through a committed and productive workforce.

While different, the concepts of management and leadership are important in their own ways. In simple terms, leadership produces change while management facilitates order.

Why is leadership so important in the age of chronic illness?

If you have read the early chapters of this book, you will no doubt be aware of the role our assumptions play in creating our typical workplace policies and procedures (i.e. management tools). Unfortunately, many of the assumptions we have about illness are no longer accurate.

If we simply look for solutions in the same outdated policies and procedures that we always have, without recognizing the fundamental changes that have taken place in the health of human beings, I believe we will ultimately be frustrated with our efforts.

Leadership, by its very nature, relies on a deep understanding of a situation and the ability to update one's perceptions and beliefs. These updated beliefs become the cornerstone of a new vision. Only then can the process of *management* can begin to take over – building an order that aligns with this new vision.

Whenever I do presentations about chronic illness and employee engagement, I find that corporate and government audiences inevitably want to know about *management:*

Things like policies, techniques and processes. I have no problem with providing people with this type of information, but I think of it as the equivalent of giving a hungry person a fish.

On the other hand, if I can make them truly *understand* the problem and energize them to overcome the barriers of bureaucracy and their own long-held beliefs, I am teaching them *how* to fish. This is leadership. The great thing about engaging a leadership dynamic is that participants are not limited to just a few *take-aways* and tips, but are emboldened to create a vision and communicate it with others. This, in turn, allows individuals and organizations to come up with new and innovative ideas of their own.

The cornerstone of trust

Two elements stand out as the foundation of any strategy when tackling chronic illness in the workplace. The first involves understanding the *nature* of chronic disease (which is the main purpose of this book). The second is trust.

To me, trust is so fundamental and so obvious a subject, that I often debate whether to include it in my writing or in my presentations to corporate clients. Of course, what is obvious to me may not be so obvious to someone else. So here is a primer on *why* trust is so important, as well as some basic information on how to develop it.

If you don't know about your employee's illness, you cannot help.

I firmly believe the main reason organizations ignore chronic illness stems from the fact that they cannot see the problem. The vast majority of these health conditions are invisible and that means you cannot tell if someone is sick just by looking at them.

Therefore organizations have to rely on their employees to inform them about any health problems that could interfere with their work. However, an employee disclosing her illness puts herself in a precarious situation. She feels she may be fired, laid-off, denied future promotion or be treated negatively by her supervisor, senior managers or even her peers. The risk she puts herself in is great, even if there are resources or alternative work arrangements that could help her to do her job better.

Unless she *trusts* the organization to act in a way that is fair and will not discriminate against her, the company will not have the opportunity to better engage her. She and her organization will become victims of presenteeism.

Trust allows for informal negotiation and better communication

When someone has an incurable and unpredictable illness they worry about their livelihood. Jobs not only provide us with money to buy food and shelter but they also bring important benefits such as medical coverage. The idea of losing these essential pillars of survival when one is most vulnerable is a scary thought.

Some of the best work accommodations come from a good faith discussion between employer and employee. In fact, when done properly, these negotiations can actually strengthen the loyalty of the employee and allow for more flexible solutions that work for both sides.

Without a foundation of trust however, the employee will assume the organization will act in its own short-term interests. This will make the employee suspicious of any negotiated offer. Combine this with the reality that people are rarely comfortable making important decisions while they are impaired by their illness, and it is hardly surprising that many employees will start consulting lawyers and may become more rigid in their demands.

Trust should be present throughout *all* the layers of a large organization. However, nowhere is trust more important than in the relationship between the employee and their direct boss.

In many organizations the employee discloses their illness to their supervisor who then notifies a senior manager and

HR person. Depending on the company, major decisions may have to go through yet an *even more* senior manager.

In these situations, it is crucial for the employee to feel that their direct supervisor "has their back" and will state the employee's case in a way that will provide for a fair solution.

How do you build trust?

Trust is a complex interaction between human beings that is built up over time. There are many ways you can build trust. Here are a few examples:

Confidentiality

Confidentiality is an integral part of trust and becomes even more important when dealing with an employee who is sick. People often want the details of their health condition kept to a minimum, with the fewest number of people involved.

When I was a manager, employees would sometimes open up about their health challenges in the course of an informal conversation. They knew I would not reveal that information unless there was a very serious and urgent reason.

If their illness required a work accommodation, I would let them know who in the company I would have to tell for that accommodation to be realized. I would also involve the employee in how it was communicated and how much information people needed to know.

Following up on what you say you will do

Do not make promises you cannot keep, but make sure you do what you say you will do. If you say you will forward a doctor's note or other documentation from the employee to the HR department or the insurance company do it in a timely fashion. There is no excuse for putting these duties off and they will crush any sense of trust if you do not act on them promptly.

Keeping communication open

Following up is vital not only in deed, but also in communication. It is important to let the employee know when you have received important documents, emails, voicemails etc. as soon as possible. A quick phone call or email (assuming they are they are actually *checking* their email) to say you have received the information will help build trust and shows you understand the importance of their situation.

Going the extra mile

I once had an employee with a short-term disability claim. She sent a doctor's note packed loosely in a large envelope that also contained a work-related package. I slid out the package and tipped the envelope upside down, but nothing else came out. The note must have been trapped underneath my finger. She had not told me the note would be in the envelope, so I tossed it in the garbage. I found out about it later that night when I spoke to her on the phone. By that time, the janitors had emptied my garbage can.

It would have been easy for me to adopt a defensive tone and admonish her for not making the presence of the note clear to me before I received it. Instead, I calmly explained what had just happened and said I understood that having her go back to her doctor was inconvenient. I offered to spend the next hour trying to find the note – even if it meant fishing through the dumpster.

I spent the next 60 minutes knee-deep in garbage but was unsuccessful. However, the employee was impressed that I would go to these lengths to help her. She got the doctor to fax a copy of the note to me the next day and told me how much she appreciated having such an understanding person as a manager. By showing both empathy and a willingness to help, I saved what could have been a trust-killing experience.

Doing the small things on a daily basis

We all know that trust is something that is built up over time. It is something that is *earned*. Respecting the confidentiality of your employees, communicating courteously and following-through on what you say you will do is not something you should start doing only when an employee is sick. For you to be trusted, these elements need to be a fundamental part of your day-to-day job as a manager. Before employees trust you with big issues, they will often test your trust will small ones. Do not neglect this daily opportunity to build trust with your employees.

Can sick people really be high performers?

"Every defeat, every heartbreak, every loss, contains its own seed, its own lesson on how to improve your performance the next time." - Malcolm X

People who live with chronic illness are no strangers to adversity. One of the things that made me so driven to succeed was that I had to overcome major obstacles in my life at an early age. In other words, my sickness made me a fighter. Looking back through history, I discovered that many great leaders had similar challenges and successfully battled through them. Here are a few:

Galileo – mental illness
Winston Churchill – depression
Albert Einstein – suspected inflammatory bowel disease
Julius Caesar – epilepsy
Charles Darwin – severe digestive illness
Sir Isaac Newton – epilepsy
Sigmund Freud – mouth cancer
Napoleon – kidney disease
Thomas Jefferson – arthritis, cluster headaches
Abraham Lincoln – depression and suspected cancer

Some more recent leaders with chronic health conditions include a trio of guys named "Steve":

Stephen Covey – ulcerative colitis
Stephen Hawking – amyotrophic lateral sclerosis
Steve Jobs - cancer

Female leaders often need to overcome challenges such as sexism to succeed. There are many who have overcome chronic illness as well. They include:

Indira Gandhi – chronic lung disease
Gloria Steinem – cancer
Frida Kahlo – polio

To be fair, you don't need to look very far to find leaders and other high performers who battle chronic illness. Chances are some of your best people have a long-term health condition you do not even know about.

The impact of multiple illnesses

Chronic health conditions tend to come in bunches. We know that people with one chronic illness will likely develop another. In fact, many people actually battle several conditions at once.

In the 2010 *Patient's Voice* survey of chronically ill workers in Canada, 73 percent of respondents reported having *more* than one chronic health condition with a significant number having *three or more* diseases. According to the study, Canadians with multiple chronic conditions:

- have twice as many consultations with a family doctor
- have 1.5 times as many consultations with specialists and other doctors
- are four times more likely to stay overnight in hospitals
- have three times more nights spent in hospitals
- have four times as many consultations with nurses
- are eleven times more likely to receive home-care services

How do multiple illnesses affect recovery?

Multiple chronic conditions can make it difficult for a person to get back on track and functional once one of the conditions starts to flare. A flare-up of one disease can often cause problems with a secondary condition. Medication must be carefully balanced. It is surprising how many medications for one illness interfere with medications for another. Some medications also have long-term side effects and these can cause further problems with both physical and mental health.

A 1992 study revealed that people with chronic health conditions are up to 20 percent more likely to suffer from depression. I know from experience that trying to overcome a physical challenge while your coping skills are impaired can be a difficult task.

Dealing with more than one illness is a lot like bringing a car out of a skid in the snow - the car fishtails one way then the other. It can take awhile to get going in the right direction again. The bottom line is that chronic conditions are often much more complex than people realize.

Exploding the lifestyle myth

We are living in an age where lifestyle is finally being recognized as one of the cornerstones of health. There are good reasons to be concerned about our lifestyle these days. As our population gets older, our bodies become more difficult to maintain and the consequences of poor lifestyle choices can become more evident.

The concept that we should be actively involved in our own health makes a lot of sense. For too long our health system has concentrated on fixing problems to the detriment of promoting wellness and I believe it is important that we address this imbalance.

The difficulty occurs when we pursue lifestyle solutions with a religious zeal, believing that lifestyle is the cause and cure of every ailment and every disease. It is true that many chronic illnesses such as type 2 diabetes, lung cancer, heart disease and hypertension often have roots related to diet, exercise or smoking. These are significant health issues that impact a large number of people and should not be ignored.

Unfortunately, we have a tendency as human beings to generalize ideas and concepts. As a result, the term chronic illness has become shorthand for *lifestyle illness*, which is fundamentally incorrect.

To put this in context, *The World Health Organization* identifies more than 70 different types of chronic illnesses and most of them are *not* directly related to obesity, lack of exercise or smoking. In fact, many of these diseases can occur in people with relatively healthy lifestyles.

When cause and effect do not apply

One of the most difficult things for healthy people to understand is that people with certain illnesses sometimes have little control over their disease. Many conditions (particularly autoimmune disorders) can flare up for no obvious reason. This is an uncomfortable truth that most people do not like to hear. As human beings we like to think we have total control over our health, but the sad fact is that sometimes we do not.

Regrettably, people with chronic illness often get blamed for things they have no control over. I have had more than one coaching client phone me in tears after being reprimanded from her boss for not taking care of herself. The employee's disease had flared up and the manager made the assumption that something the employee did or did not do was likely the cause.

The pressure to make yourself better

This idea that every person with a chronic illness is somehow responsible for their poor health is not only incorrect, but puts additional strain on someone who is already managing a great deal of stress in their lives. The resulting level of guilt and frustration can be considerable.

To add to the stress, the complex and individual nature of many chronic diseases often makes it difficult to distinguish "healthy behavior" from "non-healthy" behavior.

I remember an incident involving a friend of mine who had Crohn's disease and, like me, could no longer eat high fiber foods due scar tissue build-up on his intestines. I listened as a co-worker started criticizing my friend's diet to another person in the office; "No wonder he's always sick! Look at the crap he eats - meat, dairy and white bread."

As I overheard this unjust criticism, I couldn't help but realize that this was exactly the same diet *I* was limited to. I wondered how many people were thinking the same thing about *me* – and criticizing me behind my back.

Please keep this in mind the next time you feel compelled to give health advice to co-workers or employees. Every illness is different, and what may be healthy for you could be detrimental for them.

Making judgments about others is an unfortunate, but common aspect of our human nature. However, judging the lifestyle of someone with a chronic illness without knowing the facts is not only hurtful to the employee but could also cause damage to the organization in the long run.

Is your wellness program working as well as it could?

Wellness programs have become relatively commonplace in North American companies. Many of these programs include one or more of the following:

- Employee Assistance Program (EAP)
- Health promotion and education
- Weight management and fitness
- Stress management
- Screenings and immunization

A good wellness program has been shown to bring a significant return on investment. However, it has been my experience that they tend to be under-utilized by the people that need them the most.

A health expert once confided to me that what wellness programs do best is help keep fit people fit. A 2011 study of Canadian workers, called the *Sanofi-Aventis Healthcare Survey*, shows this is indeed the case.

According to the study, the employees *most likely* to take part in wellness programs are those who already exercise four times or more per week. The people *least likely* to participate in wellness programs are those in the 35 to 44 age group – a prime demographic for chronic health conditions.

It may be that your wellness program is simply not engaging people with chronic illness. Why would that be? Here are some possible reasons:

Your wellness program lacks diversity

I recently shared a conference table with an executive from a large company. He was a physical fitness buff and stressed the concept of fitness within his business. He had instructed the company cafeteria to ensure that all the dishes they served included vegetables and whole grains. He also insisted that members of his inner circle go jogging during lunch hour and created an aura of physical competition among his employees, using peer pressure to make sure everyone participated. While I admired the tenacity of his beliefs, I could not help but think what a nightmare his workplace would be for someone like me.

Eating high fiber items such as fruit, vegetables and whole grains would literally send me to the emergency room, and a high impact exercise like jogging would aggravate my arthritis to the point where I would barely be able to walk. In addition, having the peer pressure of living up to an ideal of healthy behavior that was actually dangerous for me would leave me feeling isolated, misunderstood and far from fully engaged.

Respecting diversity within your wellness program is a crucial part of engaging people with chronic health conditions. Everyone has different limits. If there is too much emphasis on *one way* to be healthy, people with chronic illness may stop paying attention to what the wellness program has to offer. They may also feel uncomfortable and stigmatized.

Workers are worried about their illness being revealed

Employees with chronic illness may not use company wellness programs for fear of their illness becoming known to others. Employee assistance programs, in particular, are treated with suspicion. Many workers do not believe the process is truly confidential.

Remember that these people may feel they are risking their jobs or their careers by admitting they have a health problem. The question they will ask themselves is: *Are the resources I will get through my EAP worth the risk of me losing my job?*

Unless you can convince employees they will *not* be punished for being sick, the resources that could help them will be underutilized.

Having a management team that understands chronic illness issues can build the trust needed for employees to access these programs. You can use the information at the front of this book to contact me for more details on organizing this type of training.

Your wellness program is not part of a healthy organization strategy

Employee health and wellness encompass so much more than a simple wellness program or EAP. Everything from vacation-time, workflow, and organizational culture plays a part. For instance, one of the best ways to engage employees with chronic health problems is through flexible work arrangements. Multiple studies have shown that workers with chronic illnesses rank flexible hours as the top resource that allows them to work more efficiently.

For more information on what a healthy organization entails, check out Graham Lowe's book *Creating Healthy Organizations: How Vibrant Workplaces Inspire Employees to Achieve Sustainable Success* (Rotman/UTP Publishing).

Just as healthy people are vigorous, thriving, resilient, and fit, the book shows how to foster the same healthy qualities within your organization - enabling strong links between employee wellbeing, organizational performance, and social responsibility.

Are sick days a relic of the past?

The notion of paid (or even unpaid) sick days is something that confuses me to this day. I understand the concept, but the execution is so inconsistent among organizations that the results are often ludicrous.

On one side, there are companies that offer no paid sick days at all. Some also demand a doctor's note for every single *unpaid* sick day that an employee takes off. Contrast that with other organizations, such as government or unionized workplaces, where employees can sometimes get up to 50 paid sick days a year. The problem here occurs when employees treat paid sick-days like vacation days – taking as many as the rules give them whether they are sick or not.

Frankly, neither of these situations seems workable in the long term. Having an organization that tells employees they can only get sick a few days a year, or not at all, is not realistic. It is also incredibly shortsighted and shows disrespect to both the employee and the customer. Would you like to be served by someone who has the flu or buy a product made by someone who wasn't feeling their best?

On the other hand, treating sick days as a simple commodity does not work either. It undermines the whole purpose of sick days as something that many people *need*.

So here's an idea: Let's get rid of the notion of having a set number of paid sick days per year.

If employees don't know the number of sick days they are "allowed" to take, it becomes difficult for them to justify taking advantage of the system. The organization would reserve the right to ask for a doctor's note, but would only do so based on specific circumstances or a random spot-check.

In many of today's project-type work environments tracking sick days makes little sense. For these people, their work doesn't go away when they take a sick day. It simply piles up and waits until they get back. For more and more organizations it is the *result* and the *quality* of work that matters – not the number of hours the employee puts in. If a results-oriented company like *Netflix* can stop tracking vacation time, why should we be tracking sick time?

What do you think? I know not every organization is ready for this idea, but I can imagine that many are.

Employee confidentiality, secrecy and stigma

One of the most complex and delicate areas that employers in North America have to deal with when tackling employee illness is the issue of confidentiality. It is not an area I suggest managers experiment with unless they are fully aware of, and compliant with, all relevant laws. However, it is a worthwhile subject to examine, as the secrecy that often surrounds chronic illness is not always helpful to either the employee or the organization.

To begin with, not all countries have confidentiality laws. In fact, many companies in developing nations have their own doctors. Employees are expected to visit them regularly where the state of their health is then shared, in detail, with their employers.

For many of us in North America, this arrangement is seen as an invasion of privacy. Understandably, people do not wish to share their intimate health details with their employers. There are, of course, exceptions for jobs where physical fitness is an integral part of the work or where the health problems of an employee would put others at serious risk. For the most part however, employment and privacy laws protect a worker's health information.

While the privacy of the individual is important, it can be easy to confuse confidentiality and secrecy. In a perfect world, confidentially should mean that the employee is as involved in the communication of their illness as they wish to be. If the employee does not want to share details about their health condition with anyone, that privacy should be respected. If however, they want to let certain people know about their illness, they should be allowed to do so.

I had a coaching client who managed a number of employees, many of whom knew he had a chronic illness. His condition had been stable for years, but he had a sudden relapse and ended up on short-term disability leave.

He wanted to let his employees know why he wouldn't be in the office, but his bosses told him to say nothing. His employees just came to work one day and he wasn't there – and they were given no explanation as to why. Of course, everyone will automatically accept that their boss has mysteriously disappeared right?

Predictably, the rumor mill went into high gear. There was so much secrecy surrounding the missing manager that those employees who knew he had an underlying health condition assumed he must be close to *death*. Others thought the manager had been fired or suspended. Concerned co-workers were calling him at home and he suddenly found himself defending his own reputation at a time when he should have been recuperating from his illness.

Here is the problem: *In the absence of information people will make assumptions. These assumptions may be incorrect and even harmful.*

For this reason I believe it is important for the employee to be given a say in how their absence is communicated to others.

The cost of secrecy

By keeping an absence a secret we imply there is something inherently shameful or embarrassing about it. The secrecy creates a stigma that then leads to more secrecy.

Over the years I have been advised by many people not to discuss my illness with others. They argue that my co-workers and bosses will somehow look at me as flawed or weak and will use this information against me.

Of course, by cultivating that secrecy, we inherently propagate the view that illness *is* something to be ashamed of. This attitude is what keeps many people from seeking out the resources that could help them be more productive.

Why should illness be secret?

I believe that people should be able to talk about chronic illness like they would *any* aspect of their personal lives. It is something they can choose to share if they wish it. If it is okay for an employee to let her co-workers know she needs to get home by 4pm because she has a small child, it really shouldn't be any different than if she mentions she needs to leave early for lab tests or kidney dialysis.

As our population ages, we will soon reach a point where illness affects our working lives more than young children. This is a concept we should get used to sooner rather than later and adjust our expectations appropriately.

Having an organizational culture that is open to discussing illness has several advantages:

Employee retention

For many years I was a fair-weather employee and tended to jump ship when new opportunities came up in other organizations.

Then I started working at a different company. The job was originally on-call and to be truthful I was only expecting to stay there for a few months, then move on to a higher paying job elsewhere. However, when I joined the company I soon found people, like myself, who had similar health challenges. I even worked alongside someone with the same illness who did the same type of job as me.

For the first time in the workplace, I felt surrounded by people who understood what I was going through. As a result, I stayed at that company for more than a decade and did some of the best work of my career. If my co-workers had kept their health challenges a secret, I may have never developed those strong bonds with the organization.

Increased productivity & decreased presenteeism

In one of my first stints as a manager I had a talented employee (we will call her "Dawn") who was struggling with her productivity. While her talent was obvious, previous managers had been frustrated in their attempts to increase the quantity of her output.

As it was, I was dealing with my own productivity issues at the time. There were often days when I came into work feeling less than fully alert.

I was honest with Dawn on those days and told her briefly about my illness and how it might affect my work.

She suddenly revealed that she herself had been dealing with a serious invisible illness. She had been keeping it a secret because she felt no one would understand her challenges. It turns out one of her biggest issues was balancing her doctors' appointments with her strict work schedule.

Because of her productivity issues, previous management had laid down strict rules about her being in the office from 9 to 5. This made the problem worse. As many people with chronic health conditions know, doctors, hospitals and labs have limited appointments in the evening and those spots are the first to be filled. Between Dawn's strict schedule and her desire to keep her condition a secret, her health care appointments got booked farther and father apart, meaning she wasn't getting treatment as quickly as she could. More importantly, the hours she was at work were spent worrying about her health problems and how to juggle her time. She was a walking poster for presenteeism.

It was apparent to me that this strict attendance policy was not working for her *or* the company. It was time for a change.

Her job was a creative one that did not always depend on her being in the office from 9 to 5. I made a deal with her. I gave her targets in terms of quality and quantity of her finished product, but also allowed her all the flexibility she needed to go to her doctor appointments. I also gave her advanced permission to leave work early whenever she felt tired or ill.

Now she could work without fear. She regained her passion for her job and dramatically increased both her productivity and the quality of her work.

She still had to keep track of her hours to ensure she was working the time she was paid for. She also knew she had to hit certain deadlines and work extra hours when emergencies arose. For the most part however, her schedule was flexible and this allowed her to take care of herself when she needed to. The benefits to both her and the company were substantial.

Chronic illness is a problem you cannot see

If your workers are not forthcoming about their chronic health conditions, there is no way you can help them regardless of what sort of employee wellness program you may have. They can easily become the type of worker Dawn had been – disengaged, working unproductively, and making problems worse by not taking care of themselves.

If we can lift the cloak of secrecy that surrounds chronic illness, we will ultimately be in a better position to help both people and their productivity.

Dealing with a sick employee and avoiding conflict

They say there is nothing more dangerous than a wounded animal. All animals, including humans, have evolved a flight or fight survival instinct. Being injured or sick makes the flight option more difficult. As soon as we can no longer flee from our problems we go into fight mode.

A wounded animal is concerned about its very survival and the survival of its family. Suddenly everything changes and primitive emotions take over.

When someone is diagnosed with a serious chronic illness or experiences a flare-up of their disease, their lives turn upside down. They become actively concerned about their very survival both physically and financially. It is a time when fear and emotion can trump calm rationality.

During these emotional times, a sick employee will often be fearful of losing their livelihood. Moreover, they may be extremely sensitive to everything their manager or HR person says or does. In fact, the sick employee will often judge their employer's response based on the *least* sensitive person they come into contact with.

If a supervisor is sympathetic but the HR or payroll person is rude or abrupt when discussing sick leave or disability benefits, the employee will likely conclude the company is insensitive to their situation. The employee's next thought will be that they are in immediate danger of losing their job and they will be on the defensive.

If you put yourself in the employee's position, you can quickly see how the "fight" response can take hold. The company becomes the enemy – a threat to that person's very survival. This is a response that can turn ugly for the organization, resulting in presenteeism, lawsuits, negativity in the workplace, or unnecessary disability claims.

Your best approach to an ill employee can be summed up in two words - *kind* and *gentle*. By being sincerely gentle and kind you indicate to the employee that you are a human being with some empathy for the difficulties that other human beings go through in times of great emotional stress.

Being kind and gentle does not mean talking to them like a child or someone on their deathbed - just be warm and *appropriately* friendly. If you are normally chummy with the employee, getting all cold and official will immediately put them on the defensive.

Being kind and gentle requires that you recognize the following things:

It is *not* business as usual for them

Do not treat your interaction with an ill employee like you would any other problem at work. This person may likely feel that their whole life is being shattered. Demanding quick answers from them while checking your email, or interrupting them to take another call will only brand you as insensitive and a threat to their survival. Wounded animal syndrome will quickly kick in.

Remember you are on the same team

Between the possible impact of medication and the effects of the wounded animal syndrome, the employee may seem to adopt an aggressive posture. It is a natural human impulse to respond in kind. Just realize it is not personal. They may be under tremendous strain. If they need to vent for a minute, let them.

Respond with "This must be a difficult thing for you to deal with isn't it?" Then *pause*.

Let them respond to your question. The employee may not say much more than something like "yes it is." *Pause again*. This shows you have listened to what they have said and processed it. Then you might want to finish with a phrase like, "Let's try and work together on this and we will see what we can do okay?"

If the employee feels that you understand *their* position, they will be much more likely to understand *yours*.

Your questions are not always easy for them to answer

We expect people to respond to our questions with clear, accurate and definite answers. When asking questions of a person with a serious chronic illness, there could be several reasons why you do not get clear answers:

- The employee could be in pain or on medication that dulls their brain or makes them more emotional, hyper or aggressive than usual.
- They may not totally understand their illness yet.
- Their illness may be unpredictable.
- They may be distracted by other thoughts. (*Regardless of its importance, HR paperwork can often seem trivial to people facing a life-changing illness.*)

Having been the employee in this scenario on several occasions, I can tell you that being sick is a terrible time to be answering tough questions. *Can you still do your job? When are you coming back? How long will you be off?*

Depending on the diagnosis or the progress of the illness, the most common answer may be *I don't know.*

You don't need to be a personal counselor

Being kind, gentle and understanding does not mean you need to be the employee's personal counselor. While you should give them a bit of time to talk, at a certain point you may need to end the conversation and move on.

This is where I have heard so many people drop the ball – they change their tone back to "business as usual" making the kind and gentle bit seem like an act. Keep the gentle tone while moving on to the task at hand. *"I can tell there's a lot you're dealing with right now. Let us look at how we can get this paperwork done for you as quickly as we can. What we need to do now is…"*

Empathy and understanding can help diffuse the fight mechanism – making the path back to employee productivity smoother, quicker and much less expensive for the organization in the long run.

For best results, hire an expert to train your staff. The potential return on investment is greater than you think.

Seven ways to improve employee wellness and break the stigma of chronic illness

A 2009 study from Oxford University indicates that most employees do not monitor or maintain their chronic health conditions at work. A likely reason is that many workers do not want to reveal they are sick. This means that resources that could help the ill employees are not being accessed because little or no conversation is taking place between employees and their managers.

There *are* ways to create a more open dialogue about chronic health issues in the workplace. This in turn can help employees get the resources they need to become more productive. Here are seven strategies to get you started. If you decide to incorporate any of these ideas, please remember to follow all laws related to employee privacy and confidentiality.

Awareness training

Chronic illness awareness training should start with your management and HR team. My company, *Sick with Success*®, offers programs specifically geared to corporate leaders. If your top people do not understand the issues, then they will be unable to properly communicate with their employees.

Once your organizational leaders have been trained, it is time to take your communication to the rest of the organization. In addition to formal training there are also less expensive ways to create awareness. For instance you could recognize *Invisible Illness Awareness Week, Mental Illness Awareness Week* and similar events. You can do lunch-and-learns with various health practitioners or bring in public educators from the Arthritis Society, Diabetes Association or other foundations to talk specifically about the impact of chronic diseases in the workplace.

While these events are not the be-all-and-end-all of your program, they will show employees that your organization values their health. More importantly, they send the subtle but significant message that chronic illness is something your employees can talk to you about.

Re-name your sick room

If you have an employee sick room, think about changing it to a *wellness room*. The cynical amongst you may scoff at this, but the change should include more than just a name. Send out communications reminding employees that there is a private place where they can take medication, monitor their condition or rest from dizziness or fatigue. Remember, your goal here is to get them to take care of themselves and make them comfortable doing it.

Use your committees

Perhaps you already have a health or wellness committee at work. Find ways to encourage employees with chronic health conditions to serve on these committees so that they can add their point of view. Let us not forget that chronic conditions are also known as *invisible disabilities*, so including a person like this on your diversity committee makes a lot of sense too. Again, the point here is to get a discussion going and identify possible issues that are keeping people with chronic illness from being fully engaged in the workplace.

Find a champion

We know that approximately 1 in 3 working aged North Americans have a chronic illness. That means many of your supervisors and managers will be among them. Is one of them eager to come forward to tell their story? If you can get someone who your employees admire to come out of the closet with their illness – other employees will likely follow suit. If your champion reveals how they maintain or treat their condition during the course of their workday, it will inspire others to take responsibility and do the same thing. Just remember, a champion must be a true volunteer and be comfortable sharing this information with others.

Try a buddy system

This takes the champion model to the next level. If you already have employees who are open about their illness at your workplace, ask them if they would be interested in being a buddy to someone else who is struggling with a similar problem. I can attest to the fact that working alongside people with similar health conditions makes a person feel more comfortable, confident and understood at work.

A warning though, asking people to talk about their illness with others should be done with the utmost care and confidentiality. If someone is hesitant to talk, do not force the issue or try to sell them on the idea. All you are doing here is identifying someone who they might like to talk to on their own time. Whether they follow up is up to them. They need to know this is an informal chat and not an official part of a company policy.

Use your Employee Assistance Program

Reminding *all* of your employees about the resources that are available to them is always beneficial. If these resources are confidential, stress this fact. As many employees are skeptical of EAP confidentiality, giving them a more detailed look at how EAP resources are set up and accessed will sometimes help.

Find a chronic illness coach

EAP resources may work well for some people, but often not for others. Chronic illness coaches specialize in helping people overcome their health challenges and reach their goals. More importantly, their real-life experience adds a dimension of understanding and authenticity that employees will respect.

To find out more, you can search the term *chronic illness coach* online or check out *www.sickwithsuccess.com* for more information on these specialized coaching resources.

These seven simple ideas can leverage some of the assets you already have, while incorporating some relatively inexpensive additions. Considering the costs of presenteeism and absenteeism in the workplace - specialized training and coaching could save you money in the long run.

Jason Reid

Thriving in the Age of Chronic Illness

PART III – HOW TO WORK BETTER WHEN YOU ARE SICK

Working with a chronic illness is not always easy. People with chronic health conditions often have limits in terms of energy and physical ability, but working and living smarter can frequently offset these challenges.

There are two elements to dealing successfully with a chronic condition. The first involves *maintaining* your health and *treating* your disease as well as you can. This means working with your doctor to find treatments that work for you, as well as making any changes to your lifestyle that will improve or maintain your health.

The second element is your *reaction* to the illness. How do you *feel* about yourself and your new challenges? How *flexible* are you willing to be to adapt to your new limits? How *motivated* are you to navigate through the ups and downs and uncertainty? Are you willing to go out of your comfort zone to ask for what you need?

These are tough questions, but keep in mind that your reaction to your illness and your openness to new perspectives is something within your control.

When you have a chronic condition, it is easy to focus on your limits to the point where all you can think about are the things that you can no longer do. Speaking as someone who has lived most of his life with a chronic condition, it took me a long time to understand an important fact: *Even healthy people have limits.*

While I accept that chronic pain and occasional fatigue limit me to a degree, I also realize that no one person has an inexhaustible supply of energy. In fact, a lot of people waste their energy through fear, worry, bad habits, and unhealthy relationships. These are areas largely within our control.

So here is the secret: By sorting out other areas of your life and developing clear values and goals, you will be able to take the energy you *do* have and put it towards the things that matter – the things that make you a *success,* however you wish to define that term.

Success is measured differently for everyone. Some chronic conditions are easier to cope with than others. I do not want to be unrealistic and suggest that every person with a serious health issue can earn a six-figure salary, but I am also hesitant to put limits on what you can do. There are many people who face difficult challenges and still create amazing results in their lives.

My goal is not to make you feel guilty for not accomplishing enough, but to inspire you to try new things. Building a successful career while challenged by a chronic condition can be difficult. It requires courage. But if you are reading this book, you already have that courage. This next section will give you some ideas on how to make your work life a little easier and lot more engaging.

The power of choice

A s a coach I do a lot of professional development and training to hone my craft. A major tenant of coaching is the identification of choices. During a recent workshop, I had a spirited discussion with another coach when he insisted there are some decisions in life where people don't have a choice. I argued that people *always* have a choice on some level. As proof, I told him this true story:

I was in my final year of high school when my intestine perforated. I eventually went into toxic shock and ended up in the hospital. After emergency surgery I found myself in the intensive care unit. I was flat on my back in ICU for a week. I also had a hard plastic ventilator down my throat, meaning I couldn't move my head, eat, talk or even feel myself breathe.

There was absolutely nothing I could physically do but stare at the ceiling for days on end. I could not even mark the passage of time as there were no outside windows and the fluorescent lights were on at the same brightness all day and all night.

If anyone was living a life without choice that week it was me. My external world was rigidly fixed. Minute-by-minute, hour-by-hour, day-by-day, there was nothing I could change.

Interestingly, there were changes. Sometimes I felt sad, and other times happy. There were times when I realized I was living a glorified lab experiment and found it philosophically interesting. Despite the fact my outer world remained unchanged, I realized I had quite a bit of choice in how I felt about myself.

If my thoughts focused too much on my physical limitations, I quickly felt panicked and upset. If I thought about all the wonderful things I was going to do once I got out of the hospital, I became calm, happy and even creative.

With no physical distractions in my outer world I found the rest of that week to be one of the most interesting periods I have ever experienced. I became totally immersed in my own thoughts and realized I had drastically underestimated the amount of choice I had in my life.

Thankfully, my condition was not permanent and I quickly regained my physical abilities. However I was determined to take a valuable lesson away from this unique situation. I would never again underestimate the power of choice.

How many times have you heard people use the phrase *I had no choice?* Unfortunately, human beings tend to generalize their circumstances and ignore the fact they *do* have a choice. The choice may be one-sided, or it may be difficult. We may not want to take responsibility for this choice, but it is still our choice to make.

Even if the choices in our outer-world seem limited at times, the choices of how we look at a difficult situation and react to that situation are open. We can concentrate on the lemons or see the opportunity to make lemonade.

Do I tell my prospective employer I'm sick?

If you think employers discriminate against people with chronic illness or disabilities you are right. Over the past few years, research teams have done studies by sending identical resumes and cover letters to employers - the only difference in the cover letters was a disclosure of a mental or physical illness or disability. Predictably perhaps, the resumes that had these disclosures elicited a lower response from prospective employers.

Mentioning your health condition in your resume or cover letter is probably not the best strategy, but that doesn't mean you should keep your illness hidden from your employer forever.

Start at the beginning

Before applying for a job at a particular company you might want to do some research on them. Do they have a progressive hiring policy? Do they have flexible work schedules? You should also look for any awards or citations the company may have received for their health or diversity policies.

There are many independent lists of *best employers* that can give you an insight into how a company treats its workers. Of course, there are no guarantees that you and the company will be the right fit, but being aware of an employer's reputation can allow you to target companies that may be more open minded about accommodating your illness than others.

Do you disclose your illness during the job interview?

When making the decision whether to disclose, the first question to ask yourself is whether your illness will affect your job. For example, if your health condition is relatively mild and will not require accommodations such as specialized equipment or extra sick days then you may not need to mention it.

However, if you have a condition that could affect your work at some point in the near future, it may be advisable to let your employer know. If your illness is going to affect your employment from day one, then it is probably best you disclose it right away.

In addition, there may also be issues surrounding your work-based medical insurance, particularly if you are living in the United States. You may have to disclose your illness to get proper medical coverage.

What are the benefits of disclosing your illness early on?

There are a couple of benefits to disclosing your health condition earlier rather than later. First, you can get a sense of how open and understanding the company actually is.

Finding out organizational attitudes early on can allow you to make a choice about whether you really want to work with this organization or not. It may be better to find out their attitudes now then wait until illness flares and your choices become more limited.

On the flip-side, disclosing your illness will also give the employer a chance to *help you* with possible accommodations in your work schedule or office environment.

When and how do you do it?

You could disclose your condition in the first interview, but unless your illness is obvious and visible this may not be the best time. At this point the company still does not know if your skills are the best fit for the job. On the other hand, if you wait until *after* employment letters have been signed, it might look like you were being deceptive.

Perhaps the best time to broach the topic is in the negotiation phase. At that point you know that the employer feels your skills are right for the job. By disclosing your illness *before* the paperwork is signed you are showing respect to your prospective employer, as well as demonstrating confidence in yourself and your coping abilities.

Confidence is the key attribute when discussing your illness. You show confidence by explaining your illness in a simple straightforward way. If you *do* need certain accommodations, take responsibility where you can and show them that you are a team player. *"My illness does require me to take a weekly hospital visit during business hours, but I can schedule it so I'm only an hour late for work and will make that time up by staying an hour late that day."*

Work is a team game. While your employer may be obligated to provide you with reasonable support, you have to show you are responsible for managing your condition and making sure the job gets done.

On the job

There are other circumstances where you may be required to disclose at least some information about your illness. They may include the following:

- Your employee benefit plan requires you to submit claims directly through your employer.

- Your employer has an absenteeism policy that requires you to provide a doctor's note if you miss a certain number of working days.
- You are requesting an accommodation. You will have to provide enough information to the employer so that they can properly accommodate you.

Duty to accommodate

In Canada, the United States and many other developed countries, employers are required to accommodate workers with disabilities. Generally speaking, the employer needs to make a genuine effort to accommodate the employee. Meanwhile, the employee is expected to co-operate and help facilitate a solution.

You may want to find out about specific laws that apply to your workplace. A local law society, or disability advocacy group, may be able to help you.

It is your choice

Ultimately, there are both risks and benefits to disclosing your condition. The risk is that your employer or manager may treat you differently or actively discriminate against you. The benefit is that disclosing your illness can allow your employer to provide you with the support and accommodation you need to do the job to the best of your abilities. In many circumstances, the choice of disclosure is up to you.

Developing a good relationship with your employer

When it comes to the topic of chronic illness in the workplace, discussions tend to revolve around laws, regulations and policies involving disclosure and accommodation.

While these are important, what often gets lost in the discussion is the relationship between the individual employee and the company. While there are laws and policies to protect both the worker and organization, the least stressful and most effective forms of workplace accommodation often spring from good relationships and goodwill on both sides of the divide.

To assess the amount of goodwill you have with your own organization you may want to ask yourself the following questions about your work life:

Are you normally upbeat, professional and pleasant?

Whether you are sick or well, there is no excuse for being consistently negative. If you criticize your boss, your company or your co-workers in front of others you could come across as unprofessional. Just because others may be doing it does not mean you have to join in.

What value do you bring to the company?

When we are feeling ill, it can sometimes be difficult to be the model employee, but what about your good days? Do you go above and beyond your job description? Are you on volunteer committees? Do you do things that show you really care about your work and not just about collecting a paycheck?

Do you make you manager or supervisor look good?

If you are not sure about the answer then ask yourself; "What does my boss want and how does she want it done?" It is surprising how many people do not know what their manager truly expects from them. A job description is often simply a list of duties. Each manager may have a different way of prioritizing these duties. They may also have preferences in the way their employees communicate with them (formal or informal, verbal or written etc.) The best way to find out you manager's preferences is to ask them.

Even when you are on the best of terms with your employer there are no guarantees that they will treat you fairly when your illness flares up. However, creating a good work relationship will likely reduce your stress, increase trust and may tip the scales in your favor when you ask for assistance or accommodation.

The stress of rising expectations

Does anyone member the promise of the four-day workweek? During the late 1980s futurists predicted that computers would ease our work schedules and free up much more leisure time. Of course that never happened. Instead, technology made it possible for companies to lay off workers and move jobs to countries with cheap labor.

As a result, most people in North America are working longer hours and are under more stress than ever. Many of us now live in a world where we feel we should be richer than we actually are, which in turn leads us to financial debt and more stress. More importantly, we have constant demands on our time and attention that come from the digital world of email and smart phones. As a result we are frequently left feeling bankrupt in time as well.

We are often so caught up in our day-to-day routines that we rarely get step back and look at changes in our lifestyle that can reduce our stress and increase our personal sense of wealth. This is where someone with a chronic health condition has an advantage. Becoming sick can quickly put things into perspective and help people identify what is most important to them. It also makes us more aware of the limits of human beings. There is only so fast we can go without crashing.

So what can we do to help alleviate our stress-inducing lifestyle? How do we allow the changes brought on by the digital world to make our lives a better place? The salvation of our sanity and our leisure will come when we learn to adjust our expectations and allow technology to serve us and not the other way around.

Information addiction

Are you addicted to information? When I ran a national television newsroom I was bombarded by more than a hundred emails every day. People needed my decision *now,* and with the advent of the smart-phone, I was always attached to my inbox.

After a while, I started longing for a day when I would no longer be subject to this constant stream of information. When I left television news I had my wish. My email dropped from over a hundred messages a day to less than a handful. What happened? Did I savor all of this liberated time? No. I kept checking my email at the same frequency and oddly enough became more and more anxious the less email I got. I was addicted to the data stream. Without that stream of information, I felt I must be missing something important.

Why?

My guess is that I spent years telling myself it *was* important and surrounding myself with people who thought the same way. Rather than email helping my life, my life had become my email. I needed to find a way that technology could serve *me.*

Watch what you buy

How much is your "stuff" keeping you from that enjoyable, relaxed, walk in the park? Everything from big-ticket items to digital devices can potentially add to our stress levels. The next time you buy something think of the cost in time. How much time did you have to work to get the money to buy this? How much time will *using it* take away from other things you could be doing? How much time does it cost to maintain or upgrade your purchase? It is amazing how quickly the things we buy can dominate our time.

Avoiding guilty parent syndrome

I do feel sorry for parents these days. Apparently if you don't have your child signed up for swimming lessons, French lessons, piano lessons, soccer, hockey, baseball and math camp all at once you are considered a bad parent. No doubt many of these activities are enriching, but too much of it trains our children to be like us – stressed out and obsessed with being busy. We forget how much creativity comes from having time to do nothing. Lessons teach kids to follow rules and learn tasks, but true genius often comes from having time to experiment and dream.

Time and money are two of our top stress-inducing subjects. By looking closely at our habits and lifestyles in the digital age we can find ways to free up both, becoming inherently richer and more relaxed in the process.

Seven ways to balance work and personal life

Any high-performing person knows that the secret to long-term success is a matter of balancing both your professional and personal needs. As you can imagine, this balance is even more critical for those with a chronic illness. Here are seven ways to help you find that balance.

Energy management

While simple time management is important, energy management is even more crucial. Both your physical and mental health are keys to high-performance. You need to make sure you have time to eat properly, exercise, take necessary medication or physical therapy, enjoy a hobby, as well as spend time with friends and family. You will also want to schedule time for all your healthcare appointments.

Focusing on work to the detriment of health and energy building activities can hinder your productivity in the long run.

Prioritize

Our personal lives are often as busy and stressful as our professional ones. Knowing what to spend your time and energy on is important. Take an inventory of your personal values and the things that are most important to your physical and spiritual well-being. Make time for these items first.

Learn to say no

This is part of prioritizing. There will always be demands from other people – both in your professional and personal life. Once you have decided what is important and what you can handle – learn to say no to those people you cannot accommodate.

Be realistic

People often underestimate the time it takes to do a task, travel to a meeting, or even take a break. Be realistic about how long things take and make allowances for the unexpected.

Using life hacks

Life hacks have become popular with people looking to free up time for themselves. There is even a site called *lifehacker.com* that will help you use technology to automate things you spend a lot of time doing manually. There are many simple life hacks that deal with email for instance. Have a bunch of different email addresses? Use forwarding to send them all to one place. Save time by setting up filters that directly send emails from certain people into a specific file folder. Use the auto-respond feature to let people know you only check email at certain times a day (or on certain days not at all). Let them know if it is urgent they can phone you. It is *rarely* that urgent.

One word of caution with life hacks. There is a temptation to take the time you save with life hacks and put it back into the data stream of the digital world. Don't! Take a walk. Read a book. Spend some time with your family.

Have a support structure

Having a chronic illness is a lonely proposition, as few people will understand the challenges you face. Find people you can talk to – an empathetic spouse, a close family member, someone with similar challenges or even a coach.

Be gentle with yourself

Life isn't easy, particularly when you're sick. It is natural to beat yourself up over goals you have yet to accomplish. Chronic illness is a significant challenge and you are probably handling things much better than you think you are.

These seven tips should be easy to remember, but won't always be easy to execute. Keep in mind that things will never be perfect. Avoid feeling guilty about what you are unable to do, and concentrate on areas where you can make a difference. Your life is always a work in progress.

Fighting fatigue

The belief that fatigue is something to be overcome rather than embraced for what it is (the body telling us it is time to rest) is a relatively recent phenomenon that began with the industrial revolution, and has been strengthened by our global economy and 24-hour accesses to information.

Since we cannot turn back time, how do we tackle this difficult problem? The first thing is to make sure we are maximizing our energy. It is easy to feel there is nothing we can do about fatigue, but there are many things that can help.

Find out what is causing your fatigue

Fatigue can be caused by a number of factors. Working too many hours will add to the problem, but there may also be other reasons you are feeling tired. Make sure things like your blood sugar, iron, and vitamin levels are okay.

Depression can also be a cause of fatigue. Dealing with the stress of work, plus the stress of being sick at the same time can leave us emotionally vulnerable. There are also several medical conditions that can cause fatigue and hinder sleep. The main thing is not to be complacent about it. For more than three years I slept less than four hours a night. My body and mind seemed to be constantly humming and I could not shut them off. I thought it was an unavoidable part of my life until I was diagnosed with a hyperactive thyroid. I was given some radioactive iodine therapy and it solved the problem. If only I had checked the possibility out sooner I would have spared myself years of grief.

How to get a good night's rest

Sleep is crucial to all of us. It is a time when our body repairs itself while our mind relaxes, rejuvenates and works on problems subconsciously.

In order to sleep better, health professionals recommend getting some exercise and fresh air throughout the day, as well as avoiding heavy meals and caffeine late in the afternoon or evening. Alcohol and nicotine can also hinder sleeping.

Sleep disorders

Sleep apnea is a common problem in which people stop breathing momentarily during their sleep. Those with sleep apnea can stop breathing hundreds of times a night resulting in a significant interruption of sleep patterns. If you suspect you have sleep apnea, see your doctor.

Biological rhythms

It is important to be aware of when you are at your most alert and energetic during the day. By knowing when you are best equipped to accomplish certain tasks, you can maximize the energy you *do* have and get more done.

Our level of alertness is often dictated by our biological clock. Scientists measuring both alertness and memory have shown that these two features peak for most people just before lunch then go downhill in the afternoon. Do important tasks in the morning if possible.

The consequences of overwork

When you are putting all your energy into a job, it often means you are neglecting your family. Ask yourself a few questions: *Do you laugh with your spouse and your kids every day? Do you have fun with them? Do you actively listen when they talk to you, or are you constantly thinking about the next deadline or work-project?* If you are honest with yourself you should be able to answer these questions pretty quickly.

The power of time

Nothing beats spending time with those closest to you. Time is limited, and that is why it is so precious. Make sure you spend it on those people you value the most. Actively participate in something they like and have them do the same with you. Sometimes the best moments include watching our loved ones doing something they enjoy. Do not deprive yourself or your family of these special times.

Old friends are good for the soul

In addition to spending time with your family, make sure you save some of your energy for friends as well. Old friends in particular have a way of keeping us grounded. They may have known us when we were eating paste in kindergarten or making awkward advances to the opposite sex in high school. They are not intimidated by us and tell us like it is. Smart people use their old friends to keep grounded.

Get out and enjoy life

There have been many times that I have forced myself to go to a party or other social event even though I was tired. Sometimes, I would go, feel less than social, and leave early. Other times, I found that being around people gave me more energy. Social interaction is not always an energy drain. It can keep the mind sharp and provide us with much needed stimulation.

Experiencing the natural world

We are so wrapped up in our virtual, computer-oriented lives that we sometimes forget that humans are animals who evolved, like all other animals, in a state of nature. Studies suggest that people who regularly spend time in nature tend to be happier and more relaxed than those who do not. You may find that taking a walk in the park is a good way to get some of your energy back.

The bottom line here is that *you* are in charge of prioritizing your life. You can either make time for friends, family and personal growth or risk becoming withdrawn, unhappy and ultimately unfulfilled. Life is not easy when you are sick and working a tough job, but after all, this is *your* life. If you don't make it a priority no one will.

Avoiding the extremes of denial and capitulation

Our reactions to unpredictable, long-lasting health conditions can sometimes lead to extremes. As someone who has lived with chronic illness for more than three decades, I have experienced both of these extremes and can attest to the disastrous results that follow them. For simplicity sake, we will call these two extreme reactions *denial* and *capitulation*.

Denial

Let's talk about my experience with denial first. I have always been a driven person, but chronic illness can slow even the most determined of us down. When I'm in too much of a hurry to be sick, the temptation is to ignore new symptoms and even substantial amounts of pain. I learned the hard way that this can be deadly.

When I was in my final year of high school I was determined to get good grades for university. Unbeknownst to me, just before the beginning of the school year, my intestine had perforated (split open). The pain got just a little worse every day, but every day I braced myself and went to class – determined that my illness would not slow me down.

After five months of perfect school attendance, I had finally reached my limit. I woke up one morning and could no longer stand up due to the pain. It was time to call the ambulance.

To make a long story short, I nearly died of toxic shock and needed three hours of emergency surgery to repair the damage.

I had put my health at incredible risk by not listening to the messages my body had been giving me. I was so determined to continue living normally despite my growing illness, that it had nearly killed me. Denial can be deadly.

Capitulation

You can see the inherent danger in denial, but there are also dangers in the opposite reaction – a reaction I will refer to as capitulation.

Capitulation literally means *giving up*. Here's how it works: Human beings tend to generalize, and when we find ourselves limited in the things we can do, it becomes easy for us to think we can't do *anything*.

In fact, if you find yourself automatically saying *I can't do that* to every opportunity that comes your way, you may have fallen into this trap. When you cease to push your own boundaries and continually find reasons *not* to do things in life (because your illness *might* interfere) you soon feel totally helpless.

I reached that stage in my late twenties. My health was deteriorating and I was extremely frustrated in my career. I just gave up. Looking back on it, I didn't have a bad life – I was married and lived in a condo by the ocean. Although I was underemployed I was still working as a freelance writer. I began to concentrate on my problems rather than my opportunities, feeling more and more helpless with each day. I also became intolerably bitter. I wasn't growing as a person and I wasn't learning. As a result, my mental, emotional and spiritual energy weakened and I became less and less able to cope. My confidence was gone and I was constantly negative. Not surprisingly, I lost my work, wife and condo in quick succession. Everything I had built up in my life to that point was gone. I had not reached 30 yet, but I felt my life was pretty much over. My coping skills had deteriorated to the point where I did not feel I could mentally or physically handle a regular job even if I was miraculously able to get one.

I had one thing in my favor – some money left over from my divorce. My original plan was to use that money to pay my expenses for several months and watch myself slowly go broke. However, I decided to do something different. It had always been my dream to study at one of the ancient universities in England, but I never had the money. I quickly found out I could apply for a summer term at Cambridge with the cash I had from the divorce. I decided to live my dream.

It was a bold move – something I would have done before my confidence had been leached away by helplessness and capitulation. Throwing away much needed living expenses on a university term was impractical, but just the thing I needed to push myself forward. By choosing this bold path, I felt I had made an investment in myself. For the first time in years, I felt I was growing again.

The joy and success I found in learning new things extended into other areas of my life. I soon had new friends, a renewed confidence and an optimistic outlook. Surprisingly, my health also improved. The thought of giving up on my life seemed silly now. The negative spiral I was in had stopped. When I came back to Canada, I quickly found a good job, a new place to live and new relationships. I had built my life all over again and was more confident than ever.

I hate to think what would have happened had I not chosen to re-engage my life. Giving up is an easy strategy, but ultimately an empty one that can lead to both physical and spiritual ruin.

I realize now that life with a chronic health condition will always demand some balance. We need to know when to slow down, when to take on repairs and when to travel full steam ahead. As long as we avoid the rocky shoals of both denial and capitulation, we can navigate a course that moves us forward and keeps us safe.

Jason Reid

How to think better when you are sick

In the fall of 2010, I attended a fascinating lecture on memory and cognition by Dr. Donald Stuss, a senior scientist at the *Rotman Research Institute* and an expert in the field of aging brains.

His studies indicate that our memory drops off significantly as we get older, and that deterioration starts as early as age 21. When attempting to remember something, or even solve a problem, an older brain is less efficient, despite the fact it has more knowledge at its disposal.

However, the mind has the remarkable ability to compensate for this inefficiency by engaging other parts of the brain not normally associated with memory or problem solving. The idea that our brains have the ability to "re-map" themselves is known as *neuroplasticity*.

I asked Dr. Stuss about the effects of chronic pain and fatigue on the brain. He replied that these very conditions actually mimic the same effects we see in aging. Moreover, long-term exposure to chronic pain can actually *shrink* the frontal lobes of the brain, affecting its ability to focus, reason and analyze. Of course, many of us who live with chronic pain already know this instinctively, but there are advantages to understanding *why* this is true.

Dr. Stuss says we can help ourselves stay focused even when dealing with moderate amounts of pain and fatigue. Here are some tips.

Avoid multi-tasking

Studies from Stanford University show that almost no one is good at multi-tasking, although many of us think we are. Dr. Stuss adds that multi-tasking gets more and more difficult as the brain gets older, so eliminate distractions wherever you can.

Use the morning for important tasks

Researchers found that older brains can match younger ones at cognitive function in the morning, but by afternoon the older folks rapidly decline in their ability to concentrate, while the young ones hold their own. If you are more alert in the morning, use that time to do the work that requires the most concentration.

Use association and other memory tricks

As our memory deteriorates we can make things easier for ourselves by using tricks like word association to remember important points. For instance, I developed the acronym U-ILL to make it easy to remember that chronic illness is *unpredictable*, *invisible* and *long lasting*. This makes it easier to communicate as well.

Take breaks

When I write articles for my website or for magazines, they are usually done at more than one sitting. I find that after ninety minutes my concentration starts to fade, so I switch to doing something else for a while. Sometimes I even take a short nap or meditation break to recharge my mental batteries. Dr. Stuss says taking these types of breaks can make a big difference in our ability to concentrate.

Exercise

Multiple studies have shown the beneficial affects of exercise on concentration. Eating properly and getting enough sleep also helps.

Socialize

Dr. Stuss says that socializing with people can easily rival doing crossword puzzles when it comes to keeping your brain in top shape. Social interaction is inherently unpredictable, forcing us to use parts of our brains we may not use otherwise.

Avoid negative stress

Challenging ourselves and pushing our limits can be beneficial to our brain health. However, the negative stress of constant multi-tasking, and taking on more than we can accomplish, can shrink the frontal lobes of our brain and severely impair our thinking. Are you able to think clearly when you are in a tizzy? Likely not. This is why.

Hard work pays off

Dr. Stuss says that the more effort you put into understanding and learning something, the better it sticks in your memory over the long run, giving you a depth of wisdom that can rival a young person's ability to retain more short-term information.

Like many things in life, we can look at our physically deteriorating brain as an unsolvable problem, or an opportunity to grow and enrich ourselves.

How to manage people when you are sick

Being a manager is easy. Being a successful manager is difficult. Having a vision, taking care of your employees, following company policies and delivering measurable results within a fixed amount of time is not something everyone can accomplish.

For several years I managed a creative group of people across a large country in a challenging competitive environment with stringent hourly and daily deadlines. I was on-call 24-hours a day, seven days a week. I succeeded in my job despite the challenges of a painful chronic illness that made me less than my best… well… most of the time actually.

Despite my physical limitations and the challenges of the job, I ran a successful department - nearly quadrupling our output in less than five years and winning major awards. I cannot begin to describe the satisfaction of leading a group of talented people and helping them be their best. They responded by helping me get through more than a few rough patches when my energy was low and my health was poor.

It is my belief that people are not "human resources". They are people. They have individual personalities and needs. This is what makes managing people challenging, particularly when you are fatigued, or in pain.

So how do you manage your employees when you are going through a period of illness? Well one of the best solutions is to manage your people well *before* you need their help. Here is how:

Put together a successful team

As managers we are not expected to do it all. We are supposed to manage *others* to do the bulk of the work for us. Some managers avoid hiring exceptional workers because they worry that star employees will become their competition. I have always felt that this way of thinking was silly. If your employees do their work well, they will make you look good. If you do nothing else but find and hire exceptional people you can be a successful manager.

Hiring good people does not have to be overly expensive. Exceptional people are not always the ones with the most experience or the highest salary expectations. Find people that can understand a vision and execute a plan.

Allow them to work independently

Is your department so policy driven that your employees have to ask permission to do anything that deviates in the slightest from the norm? If so you are not really a manager but an operator of machinery. Give your people some space to think things out themselves. This will help take the pressure off you when you are ill.

Provide a vision

If you provide a consistent vision and articulate it daily, you need not fear your employees' decision-making abilities. For instance, my news reporters always knew that I was ideally looking for people-oriented stories, told in a conversational style with bonus points for original ideas and diversity. By being explicit with my vision, my reporters did not need to ask me many questions. They knew what I wanted. They also knew they had the ability to go outside those parameters if they were truly inspired to do something creative and original. I gave them permission to fail and backed them up if things did not work out.

Establish good relationships

Permission to fail is one of many ways of developing good relationships with your employees. These relationships will ultimately make it easier for you when you *do* get sick. If your employees trust you and feel you have their back, they will appreciate the opportunity to do something positive for *you* when the opportunity arises.

Be honest (to a point)

If you have one or two leaders in your department who you trust (and why shouldn't you trust them if they are your leaders?) it might benefit you to be honest with them on days when you are not feeling that great. This is a tricky process, as you don't want to get them *too concerned* about you. That being said, having one of your people run some interference for you on a day you're not feeling well can help you out immensely.

Establish a preferred method of communication

For me, email was perfect after-hours "what do you think of this?" type of communication. After a long day at work I really didn't want to speak to people at night unless it was something that demanded the personal touch. Being able to text "I love that idea" or "do it" was a pretty easy solution.

So let us review. You have hired good people who can work independently. You have provided them with a vision, which means they know what kind of work you expect of them. You have developed a trusting relationship and provided an excellent work environment. You have also set out a preferred way of communication, so your employees know the best way to reach you with the minimum of effort on your part.

Once you have established this type of environment, the work will get done even if you are not there to constantly oversee it. Moreover, your employees should feel both engaged and empowered, allowing you to manage your energy even when the gas tank gets low.

Small business owners and human sustainability

If one word were to encapsulate the dilemma of the 21st century, it would be *sustainability*.

We are entering a period where the energy that drives our economy, cheap oil, is beginning to dry up. Future generations may look back at us and wonder what we were thinking in consuming such massive amounts of a non-renewable resource. After all, how can we sustain any endeavor when we use our limited energy recklessly and without thought?

With that in mind, how many of us have considered *our own* limited amounts of energy and personal sustainability?

A 2007 *Ipsos-Reid* study shows that close to half of the small business owners in Canada worked more than 53 hours a week. Many of their employees also work equally long hours.

It is tempting, in our competitive world, to view work as a sprint. We keep going a little bit faster and faster still, all the while ignoring signs of fatigue and wear. We race to get project *A* done, only to have it replaced by project *B* and Project *C*. Sprinting to get a project done is not necessarily bad, but when people have no breaks in which to rest and recuperate the sprinting pace will not be sustainable in the long run.

Having a sustainable organization is not just about using external energy wisely – it is about using human energy just as carefully and thoughtfully.

It is important to remember that human bodies are highly complex machines and they need proper fuel, maintenance and down time to be at their most efficient. It is natural to push yourself on occasion in order to get an important project done. Over the long term however, driving yourself consistently beyond your physical limits is about as smart as revving a car engine without any motor oil in it.

When it comes to maximizing your limited energy, one of the best tools is a simple time-log. In it you log how many hours you are working and exactly how those hours are being spent. There are many benefits to doing time-logs. Your organization may be spending too many hours dealing with small, problem clients or doing tasks that could easily be outsourced or automated. Fixing these issues and letting go of problem customers may not only help with stress and sustainability issues, but also benefit the bottom line as well.

What advantages do you have?

Dr. Milton H. Erickson was a remarkable man. He was an incredibly successful psychiatrist and therapist who helped thousands of people whose emotional conditions were considered un-curable. Erickson also pioneered an elegant and insightful form of hypnosis which is still widely used in areas such as psychotherapy, neurolinguistic programming and performance coaching.

The influence Erickson had on so many of these disciplines is all the more remarkable considering he fought a devastating illness nearly all of his life. Not only did he succeed *despite* his health conditions, he *used them* to his advantage.

Born in Nevada at the turn of the last century, Erickson contracted polio when he was 17. He overheard the doctor tell his parents that he was going to die, and became determined to beat the disease.

Totally paralyzed, he slowly began to re-train each of his muscles by concentrating on memories of how they used to work. Eventually, he was able to regain control of his entire body and embarked on a thousand mile canoe trip without a cane. In his later years he would suffer post-polio syndrome and use self-hypnosis to deal with excruciating pain.

His story becomes more remarkable when you learn about the development of his greatest skills – the ability to listen attentively, and to "read" people (their micro-expressions and body movement).

These skills were practiced and refined during long periods when Erickson was paralyzed and confined to bed. Looking for something to occupy his mind, he watched his family intently, searching for clues to how human beings use non-traditional communication such as body language and tone of voice. He realized that people communicated quite a bit this way even when they were not aware of it.

Eventually, he came to notice that states of mind such as wonderment, confusion and deep concentration were really forms of hypnotic trance. Once a person was in that trace, it was much easier to communicate with their unconscious mind in a positive way. He used this to great advantage in his psychotherapy practice, becoming the most celebrated and successful therapist of his time and possibly all of history.

He did all this by taking advantage of his circumstances. Paralysis is not something most of us would consider a positive experience, but for Erickson, it sowed the seeds of his greatness.

That begs the question: What possible advantages can you find in *your* situation that could make you a better person or a better employee?

Do you want to be happy or to be right?

"Bitterness is like drinking a cup of poison and waiting for the other person to die."

When I was in university, I became friends with a fellow I will call "Gary". He and I were the same age, had the same interests and had a similar upbringing and home life.

There was one difference however. Gary's parents had been born elsewhere. They had escaped a place of poverty and injustice where their people had been a suppressed minority with few rights and a long list of grievances against the government.

Gary's family had moved to Toronto when Gary was a small child. He grew up highly intelligent and had a nice way with people. He had a great future ahead of him, but then something happened.

Gary went back to visit his homeland. There he saw for himself the injustice and the poverty and the needless self-destruction of his people. When he came back home some months later he was never the same.

Overcome with bitterness, he became consumed by his outrage at the considerable issues that his people faced. He had a right to be upset, he told us. His people had been treated badly. So badly, in fact, that he took it all quite personally.

He became so bitter that he unconsciously searched for unfairness in the world around him. He went through job after job, never rising close to the level of his potential. No matter where he worked, he would eventually discover something about the organization that he considered unfair. Gary would then rebel, either openly or passively, which usually resulted in his termination or resignation.

With every year and every new job, the unfairness of the world seemed to compound itself in Gary's eyes, to the point where he stopped taking care of himself. Procrastination, addiction and self-sabotage would eventually ruin a man who once had infinite promise.

Even as his own life suffered, Gary clung tightly to his righteous indignation. Evils that he had not even experienced first-hand continued to consume him. He was right to be angry and he was right to be upset. He was so right in fact; he made himself a martyr for a cause that he could never help because he had weakened himself with this self-destructive bitterness.

Do *you* cling to a hurt or an unfairness? Many of us do, especially those of us who have been affected by chronic health conditions. You may feel you are totally right to be bitter and resentful – and that may be the case. But how is that attitude affecting you, and the people around you? Will destroying yourself change the world for the better?
Do you want to be happy or do you want to be right?
Sometimes it's a choice we have to make.

Final thoughts

If you have read through this book and had a few *a-ha* moments or times when you have said to yourself, "I hadn't thought of it *that* way before," then I feel I have done my job.

Changing our beliefs and perceptions is an important first step in any transformation. The assumptions we have about illness are so engrained that even people who *live* with chronic conditions seldom grasp the realization that they are trying to conform to an outdated idea of illness which no longer matches their reality. Chronic illness is not like having the flu, and living in a society that treats it that way can make us feel frustrated, cynical and disengaged.

We now have a critical mass of people who suffer from chronic health conditions and part of my mission is to help these people identify with others who have similar challenges.

This new *Age of Chronic Illness* affects so many aspects of our lives and our economy, that this book merely scratches the surface of some of the issues we have to address.

There are many additional books that can be written on this topic and I plan to write a few more myself. For those of you interested in reading my newest material please visit my website (*www.sickwithsuccess.com*). I have a great selection of free articles, ebooks and information that are updated regularly. You can even sign up to get my latest articles sent directly to your email inbox.

For those of you who are interested in learning more about coaching, training, or hiring me as a speaker, you can find additional information on my website or simply write me at *jason@sickwithsuccess.com*

I encourage you to send me an email and share your own stories about working with chronic illness. I look forward to hearing from you.

Glossary of terms

Accommodation: Workplace assistance. Many workplaces are required to make reasonable accommodations for people with chronic health conditions and disabilities. Accommodations could include anything from ergonomic and assistive devices to a flexible work schedule.

Acute illness: A disease with an abrupt onset and relatively short duration. The word *acute* means urgent or intense. Acute illnesses are often visible, predictable and temporary. Also see *traditional illness* or *infectious disease*.

Age of Chronic Illness: A phrase denoting the substantial impact that chronic illness is having and will have on our economy and society in the coming decades. It also signifies the dramatic change in the concept of illness overall as chronic health conditions overtake acute diseases.

Arthritis: A disorder that involves inflammation of the joints. There are many different types of arthritis with varying symptoms and treatments. A 2004 study in *The Journal of Occupational and Environmental Medicine,* indicated that arthritis was associated with one of the highest presenteeism costs per employee compared with other chronic diseases.

Autoimmune disease: Autoimmune diseases involve an overactive immune response against substances and tissues normally present in the body. In other words, the body attacks its own cells. Common autoimmune diseases include arthritis, Crohn's disease, lupus, and multiple sclerosis.

Capitulation: The act of surrendering or giving up. One of the extreme reactions to chronic illness, the other being *denial*.

Chronic health condition: See *chronic illness*.

Chronic illness: A disease of long duration. Chronic illnesses are often invisible, unpredictable and long lasting, the opposite characteristics of *acute illness* or *traditional illness*. Chronic illnesses affect more than half the population of North America with a third of those affected being working-aged.

Coaching: The practice of taking a client through the process of achieving a personal or professional goal.

Chronic illness coach: A person who practices the art of *coaching* to help a client achieve goals related to living and working with *chronic illness*. The chronic illness coach may also act as a *consultant* depending upon the situation. Coaching sessions and consultations can often be done over the phone.

Cognition: This refers to a person's mental abilities including perception, memory, learning, and problem solving.

Consultant: A professional who provides professional or expert advice.

Crohn's disease: An inflammatory disease that may affect any part of the gastrointestinal tract causing a wide variety of symptoms including abdominal pain, weight loss, fatigue, and lack of concentration. Also see *autoimmune disease*.

Demographics: This refers to the statistical characteristics of a population, including age, gender, disability and other factors.

Denial: A refusal to accept or believe something. People can sometimes show denial about the seriousness of their illness, ignoring warning signs such as intense pain.

Disclosure: The act of revealing something that is unknown. Disclosing your illness at work involves letting your supervisor or someone else in authority know about your condition.

EAP: An *Employee Assistance Program*. These programs help employees and their families manage issues in both their work and personal lives. EAP counselors usually provide assessment, support, and sometimes referrals to additional resources. An EAP's services are usually free and are also subject to privacy laws. They are sometimes also known as *EFAPs or Employee Family Assistance Programs*.

Engagement: The act of being fully involved and enthusiastic about a job or task. An *engaged employee* will usually act in a way that furthers their organization's interests.

High performer: A goal-oriented person who is able to produce consistent positive results.

Hypnosis: An artificially induced state of relaxation and concentration in which deeper parts of the mind become more accessible. Hypnosis can be used to reduce pain, work out personal issues, increase performance and decrease stress. It can be used in a clinical setting by medical doctors or, less formally, by a trained practitioner.

Infectious disease – a contagious illness caused by bacteria or viruses. Also see *acute illness* or *traditional illness.*

Leadership: The process of social influence in which a person engages others in the accomplishment of a common goal.

Life hacks: Productivity tricks originally used by computer programmers to cut through information overload and organize data. The phrase now refers to anything that solves an everyday problem in a clever or non-obvious way.

Mental health professional: A health care practitioner who offers services for the purpose of improving an individual's mental health, or to treat mental illness. These can include psychiatrists, psychologists, social workers or other licensed professionals.

Neurolinguistic programming: Also known as NLP, neurolinguistic programming explores the relationships between how we think, how we communicate and our patterns of behavior and emotion. While controversial in the scientific world, many elements of NLP are widely used in performance coaching, business and advertising.

Neuroplasticity: Our ability to have unused parts of our brain take over functions normally done by other areas of the brain. Also known as *brain plasticity.*

Neuroscience: The scientific study of the nervous system.

Organization: A group of people who work together in a structured way for a shared purpose. These can include small businesses, corporations, non-profit entities, co-operatives, or government.

Organizational leader: A person who shows *leadership* in an organization. Because organizational leaders use their ability to influence people as a tool to bring about change, they are commonly thought of as executives, managers and supervisors. However, anyone with influence in an organization can be a leader, regardless of their job title.

Paradigm: A philosophical or theoretical framework. Our traditional paradigm of illness is largely based on assumptions that disease is visible, predictable and temporary. The new paradigm of illness assumes that diseases can be invisible, unpredictable and long lasting.

Presenteeism: The act of someone showing up for work but not being fully productive. This may be due to fatigue, pain or other diminished ability caused by illness.

Psychotherapy: The treatment of mental and emotional disorders through the use of psychological techniques.

ROWE: A *Results Oriented Work Environment*. Developed originally by managers at *Best Buy*, it is a work environment where the emphasis is on the quantity and quality of work done rather than the number of hours of work and where those hours are spent (at home or at the office).

Stigma: A mark of disgrace or shame associated with a particular circumstance. People will sometimes feel discredited or isolated by others when their illness is revealed. In the context of work, people feel their abilities will be overshadowed by their illness. Repercussions at work could include termination, lack of opportunity, social isolation or other factors.

Support group: A place for people to give and receive both emotional and practical support as well as to exchange information about a common problem.

Traditional illness: See *acute illness* or *infectious disease.*

Wellness program: A comprehensive health program designed to maintain a high level of wellbeing of its participants through proper diet, exercise, stress management, and illness prevention.

World Health Organization: The health arm of the United Nations system responsible for providing leadership on global health matters. Also known as *WHO.*

References

Center for Studying Health System Change. (2009). Washington DC.

(2005). *Chronic Disease, a Public Health Issue.* Canadian Coalition for Public Health in the 21st Century.

David M. Dawson M.D., A. L. (2008). *Boosting Your Energy.* Harvard Health Publications.

DeVol, R., & Bedroussian, A. (2007). An Unhealthy America: The Economic Burden of Chronic Disease - Charting a New Course to Save Lives and Increase Productivity and Economic Growth,. The Milken Institute.

Fehmidah, M., & Hafiz, T.A. (2009, January). Health behaviours among older and younger workers with chronic illness. *Working Paper 109.*

Ipsos-Reid. (2007). *Small Business Ownership Fun, but Long Hours.* HP Canada, reviewed by Canadian Federation of Independent Business.

Kotter, J. (1990). *A Force for Change: How Leadership Differs from Management.* The Free Press.

Logan, D., & Zaffron, S. (2009). *The Three Laws of Performance.* Jossey-Bass.

Logan, D., King, J., & Wright, H. F. (2011). *Tribal Leadership Leveraging Natural Groups to Build a Thriving Organization.* Harper Business.

Lowe, G. (2010). *Creating Healthy Organizations.* Rotman UTP.

(2010). *Patient's Voice Survey.* Rogers Business and Professional Publishing Research Group.

Patra, J., Popova, S., & Rehm, J. (2007). *Economic Cost of Chronic Disease in Canada 1995-2003.* Prepared for the Ontario Chronic Disease Prevention Alliance and the Ontario Public Health Association.

(2007). *Preventing and Managing Chronic Disease.* Ontario (Canada) Ministry of Health and Long-Term Care.

Stuss, D. (2010, 09 21). Canadian Society for Training and Development workshop. *Bain Plasticity: Can we teach people to use their brains more effectively?* (J. Reid, Interviewer)

(2011). *The Sanofi-Aventis Healthcare Survey.* Rogers Business and Professional Publishing Group.

Resources

Allergies and Asthma
Allergy/Asthma Information Association
295 The West Mall, Ste. 118
Toronto, ON M9C 4Z4
T: 416-621-4571, 1-800-611-7011
Website: www.aaia.ca
E-mail: admin@aaia.ca

Asthma Society of Canada
2306-4950 Yonge St.
Toronto, ON M2N 6K1
T: 416-787-4050, 1-866-787-4050
F: 416-787-5807
Website: www.asthma.ca
www.asthma-kids.ca
E-mail: info@asthma.ca

ALS
ALS Society of Canada
3000 Steeles Ave. E., Ste. 200
Markham, ON L3R 4T9
1-800-267-4ALS [4257]
Website: www.als.ca
E-mail: iwp@als.ca

Arthritis
The Arthritis Society
1700-393 University Ave.
Toronto, ON M5G 1E6
T: 416-979-7228, 1-800-321-1433
F: 416-979-8366
Website: www.arthritis.ca
E-mail: info@arthritis.ca

Brain Tumour
Brain Tumour Foundation of Canada
301-620 Colborne St.
London, ON N6B 3R9
T: 519-642-7755, 1-800-265-5106
F: 519-642-7192
Website: www.braintumour.ca
E-mail: braintumour@braintumour.ca

Cancer
Canadian Breast Cancer Network
300-331 Cooper St.
Ottawa, ON K2P 0G5
T: 613-230-3044, 1-800-685-8820
F: 613-230-4424
Website: www.cbcn.ca
E-mail: cbcn@cbcn.ca

Canadian Cancer Society
200-10 Alcorn Ave.
Toronto, ON M4V 3B1
T: 416-961-7223, 1-888-939-3333
F: 416-961-4189
Website: www.cancer.ca
E-mail: ccs@cancer.ca

Colorectal Cancer Association of Canada
204-60 St. Clair Ave. E.
Toronto, ON M4T 1N5
T: 416-920-4333, 1-877-50-COLON
F: 416-920-3004
Website: www.colorectal-cancer.ca
E-mail: information@colorectal-cancer.ca

The Leukemia & Lymphoma Society of Canada
804-2 Lansing Sq.
Toronto, ON M2J 4P8
T: 416-661-9541, 1-877-668-8326
Info Resource Centre:
1-800-955-4572
F: 416-661-7799
Website: www.lls.org/canada
E-mail: laila.ali@lls.org

Lymphoma Foundation Canada
16-1375 Southdown Rd., Ste. 236
Mississauga, ON L5J 2Z1
T: 905-822-5135, 1-866-659-5556
F: 905-814-9152
Website: www.lymphoma.ca
E-mail: info@lymphoma.ca

Ovarian Cancer Canada
101-145 Front St. E.
Toronto, ON M5A 1E3
T: 416-962-2700, 1-877-413-7970
F: 416-962-2701
Website: www.ovariancanada.org
www.ovairecanada.org
E-mail: info@ovariancanada.org

Prostate Cancer Canada
306-145 Front St. E.
Toronto, ON M5A 1E3
T: 416-441-2131, 1-888-255-0333
F: 416-441-2325
Website: www.prostatecancer.ca
E-mail: info@prostatecancer.ca

Celiac Disease
Canadian Celiac Association
204-5170 Dixie Rd.
Mississauga, ON L4W 1E3
T: 905-507-6208, 1-800-363-7296
F: 905-507-4673
Websites: www.celiac.ca
www.celiacguide.org
E-mail: info@celiac.ca

Cerebral Palsy
Ontario Federation for Cerebral Palsy
104-1630 Lawrence Ave. W.
Toronto, ON M6L 1C5
T: 416-244-9686, 1-877-244-9686
F: 416-244-6543
Website: www.ofcp.on.ca
E-mail: info@ofcp.on.ca

Crohn's and Colitis
Crohn's and Colitis Foundation of Canada
600-60 St. Clair Ave. E.
Toronto, ON M4T 1N5
T: 416-920-5035, 1-800-387-1479
Website: www.ccfc.ca
E-mail: ccfc@ccfc.ca

Cystic Fibrosis
Canadian Cystic Fibrosis Foundation
601-2221 Yonge St.
Toronto, ON M4S 2B4
T: 416-485-9149, 1-800-378-2233
Website: www.cysticfibrosis.ca
E-mail: info@cysticfibrosis.ca

Diabetes
Canadian Diabetes Association
1400-522 University Ave.
Toronto, ON M5G 2R5
T: 416-363-3373,
1-800-BANTING [226-8464]
F: 416-363-3393
Website: www.diabetes.ca
E-mail: info@diabetes.ca

Diabète Québec
8550 boul. Pie-IX, Ste. 300
Montreal, QC H1Z 4G2
T: 514-259-3422, 1-800-361-3504
F: 514-259-9286
Website: www.diabete.qc.ca
E-mail: info@diabete.qc.ca

Juvenile Diabetes Research
Foundation
2550 Victoria Park Ave., Ste. 800
Toronto, ON M2J 5A9
T: 647-789-2009, 1-877-CURE-533
F: 416-491-2111
Website: www.jdrf.ca
E-mail: general@jdrf.ca

Epilepsy

Epilepsy Canada
336-2255B Queen St. E.
Toronto, ON M4E 1G3
T: 1-877-734-0873
F: 905-764-1231
Website: www.epilepsy.ca
E-mail: epilepsy@epilepsy.ca

Hearing Loss

The Canadian Hearing Society
271 Spadina Rd.
Toronto, ON M5R 2V3
T: 416-928-2500, 1-877-347-3427
TTY: 416-964-0023, 1-877-347-3429
F: 416-928-2523
Website: www.chs.ca
E-mail: info@chs.ca

Heart Disease

Hypertension Canada National Office
3780 14th Ave.
Markham, ON L3R 9Y5
T: 905-943-9400
F: 905-943-9401
Website: www.hypertension.ca
E-mail: admin@hypertension.ca

Heart and Stroke Foundation of Canada
1402-222 Queen St.
Ottawa, ON K1P 5V9
T: 613-569-4361
Website: www.heartandstroke.ca
E-mail: emelnick@hsf.ca

HIV/AIDS
Canadian AIDS Society
800-190 O'Connor St.
Ottawa, ON K2P 2R3
T: 613-230-3580, 1-800-499-1986
F: 613-563-4998
Website: www.cdnaids.ca
E-mail: casinfo@cdnaids.ca

Huntington's Disease
The Huntington Society of Canada
400-151 Frederick St.
Kitchener, ON N2H 2M2
T: 519-749-7063, 1-800-998-7398
F: 519-749-8965
Website: www.huntingtonsociety.ca
E-mail: info@huntingtonsociety.ca

Kidney Disease
The Kidney Foundation of Canada
300-5165 Sherbrooke St. W.
Montreal, QC H4A 1T6
T: 514-369-4806, 1-800-361-7494
F: 514-369-2472
Website: www.kidney.ca
E-mail: info@kidney.ca

Liver Disease

Canadian Liver Foundation
1500-2235 Sheppard Ave. E.
Toronto, ON M2J 5B5
T: 416-491-3353, 1-800-563-5483
F: 416-491-4952
Website: www.liver.ca
E-mail: clf@liver.ca

Lupus

Lupus Canada
3555 14th Ave., Unit 3
Markham, ON L3R 0H5
T: 905-513-0004, 1-800-661-1468
F: 905-513-9516
Website: www.lupuscanada.org,
E-mail: info@lupuscanada.org

Mental Health

Anxiety Treatment and Research Centre
St. Joseph's Hospital
301 James St. S., 6th floor
Fontbonne Building
Hamilton, ON L8P 3B6
T: 905-522-1155 ext. 33697
Website: www.anxietytreatment.ca

Canadian Mental Health Association
Phoenix Professional Building
303-595 Montreal Rd.
Ottawa, ON K1K 4L2
T: 613-745-7750
F: 613-745-5522
Website: www.cmha.ca
E-mail: info@cmha.ca

Canadian Psychiatric Association
701-141 Laurier Ave. W.
Ottawa, ON K1P 5J3
T: 613-234-2815
F: 613-234-9857
Website: www.cpa-apc.org
E-mail: cpa@cpa-apc.org

Canadian Psychological Association
702-141 Laurier Ave. W.
Ottawa, ON K1P 5J3
T: 613-237-2144, 1-888-472-0657
F: 613-237-1674
Website: www.cpa.ca
E-mail: cpa@cpa.ca

Mood Disorders Society of Canada
3-304 Stone Road W., Ste. 736
Guelph, ON N1G 4W4
T: 519-824-5565
F: 519-824-9569
Website: www.mooddisorderscanada.ca
E-mail: info@mooddisorderscanada.ca

The Organization for Bipolar Affective Disorders Society
1019 7th Ave. SW.
Calgary, AB T2P 1A8
T: 403-263-7408, 1-866-263-7408
Website: www.obad.ca
E-mail: obad@obad.ca

Schizophrenia Society of Canada
100-4 Fort St.
Winnipeg, MB R3C 1C4
T: 204-786-1616, 1-800-263-5545
F: 204-783-4898
Website: www.schizophrenia.ca
E-mail: info@schizophrenia.ca

Multiple Sclerosis
Multiple Sclerosis Society of Canada
700-175 Bloor St. E., North Tower
Toronto, ON M4W 3R8
T: 416-922-6065, 1-800-268-7582
F: 416-922-7538
Website: www.mssociety.ca
E-mail: info@mssociety.ca

Osteoporosis
Osteoporosis Canada
301-1090 Don Mills Rd.
Toronto, ON M3C 3R6
T: 416-696-2663, 1-800-463-6842
Website: www.osteoporosis.ca
E-mail: info@osteoporosis.ca

Parkinson's Disease
Parkinson Society Canada
316-4211 Yonge St.
Toronto, ON M2P 2A9
T: 416-227-9700, 1-800-565-3000
F: 416-227-9600
Website: www.parkinson.ca
E-mail: general.info@parkinson.ca

Thyroid Disease
Thyroid Foundation of Canada
803-1669 Jalna Blvd.
London, ON N6E 3S1
T: 519-649-5478, 1-800-267-8822
Website: www.thyroid.ca

About the author

Jason Reid is an expert on chronic illness and engagement. He is also a professional coach and keynote speaker.

Diagnosed at a young age with both Crohn's disease and arthritis, Jason overcame these challenges to become the news director at a national television network. There he dramatically increased productivity while leading his team to several prestigious journalism awards.

Aware that there were many ambitious people who, like himself, struggled with chronic illness issues, Jason created *Sick with Success*® - an organization dedicated to helping people with chronic health conditions thrive and be fully engaged in their lives and careers.

Jason also works with businesses and other organizations, giving them the tools to improve productivity by better engaging employees with chronic health problems. His leadership program, *Thriving in the Age of Chronic Illness,* is the first of its kind.

Jason's real-world experience gives him a unique perspective on how chronic illness affects organizations and individuals. In addition to his own experience, he has also consulted with experts in wide-ranging fields such as neuroscience, project management and motivational psychology in order to understand how people with health challenges can be more productive and engaged in today's fast-paced world.

Jason writes regularly on the topic of chronic illness and engagement for several publications and has appeared as a guest expert on Canadian television.

For additional books, or to hire Jason as a coach or speaker, please contact:

Sick with Success®
663 Montbeck Cr.
Mississauga, ON
L5G 1P1
Canada

Tel: 905.891.3584
email: info@sickwithsuccess.com
URL: www.sickwithsuccess.com

Jason Reid